Be a Shark: The Secret Sauce to Winning in Life after High School

Matthew J Wright

Copyright © 2025 Matthew J. Wright

All rights reserved.

ISBN: 979-8-218-72742-0

DEDICATION

Sharks Everywhere Making the World a Better Place

CONTENTS

	Acknowledgments	1
1	Be A Freaking Shark!	3
2	Why Sharks?	9
3	It's More Than One Number, It's Grit?	19
4	Hustling In College	24
5	Mastering Sharkyness	31
6	Networking	38
7	Bite Through Red Tape! – Be Persistent	45
8	Hunt In Groups – Build Your Teamwork Skills	55
9	Orders Of Thinking	67
10	Be Relentless	75
11	What To Study?	80
12	Finding Jobs	87
13	Be A Shark: The Game	92
14	Conclusion	95

ACKNOWLEDGMENTS

The "Be A Shark" idea and workshop has been building for years. There have been so many wonderful people who have encouraged me along the way. Lewis Nordin Jr. and Brad Conrad stand out as the two people who believed in this the most when it was the youngest. They helped it grow into something more.

The "Be A Shark" board game has had input from many different folks, from former students to groups of friends from high school. I can't tell you the endless hours we spent playing that game, laughing at one another, and tweaking the Be a Shark idea!

During this whole process, I became a Career Mentor Fellow at the American Physical Society (APS). This group within the APS, run by Midhat Farooq, is specifically designed to help physics students develop their career trajectories. I still value the training and connections this group has provided, and still participate with this group at conferences whenever I can.

The creation of the Be a Shark workshop has brought me a deeper connection to the Society of Physics Students. I especially value running the Be a Shark workshop at their conferences and gradually taking on a leadership role within their organization.

There have been a number of people who have been so helpful in preparing this book, including Brad Conrad, Nicole Franco, Natalie Ion, Kayla Stephens, and Colleen Wright. Their direct help made this book happen.

Finally, you can't do anything without a strong team at home keeping you on track. My loving and beautiful bride Colleen and brilliant and talented kid EmmaRose Soul keep me learning and innovating with their love, encouragement, and example. The continued support I get from my parents, family, and friends makes me feel like I am a shark and can accomplish anything.

PART ONE: INTRODUCTION

1 BE A FREAKING SHARK!

Whether you want to be a mechanic, mechanical engineer, doctor, nurse, or entrepreneur, you are going to consistently run into obstacles and challenges. Whether you are rich or poor, you are going to have to work hard to be successful in today's world as not only are we are in competition with everyone else, but we are also in competition with computers that can process faster than we can. But don't fear, I know the secret sauce that can propel you into an amazing career. As you read this book, I am going to show how to be successful. There is a method to the madness, and I call it being a Shark.

Since 2012, I have been blessed to be a physics professor and met some of the most remarkable people in the world – my students. I say that because many of these people I have taught have gone on to international fellowships and elite universities for graduate schools and medical schools. They have gone on to be physicists, engineers, doctors, and neurobiologists; they are every bit as **impressive** as you can imagine – and so are you.

Every year I also get to meet families of young students who are considering where they're going to go for college, and as you can imagine, high school students want to go on and have a successful career. To be somebody who makes a difference in the world around them. The parents are even more excited. And what's most important for many parents is that their child is financially stable and an asset instead of a liability in their own long-term financial situation. Sadly, some of these students – more than you think – don't make it.

The stakes are high! At the same time, this shit should be easy. It was easy in high school. It should be easy in college or on the job market, shouldn't it? I'm sorry. It ain't.

Be A Shark

There are a lot of factors that go into whether or not a high school student who is transitioning into college will go on to transition into a promising career opportunity when they graduate. As I have learned, it is a very difficult thing to predict and to get a sense of whether or not somebody's going to have ultimate success or not. I am sure this feels like a huge mountain to climb for you and your peeps! So just go get help from someone who knows right? Even when you go to get the extra help, it doesn't always work. There must be something more.

What I have learned is that to be successful as a student it helps to have a strong academic background. But more importantly, successful students also need the desire and ability to quickly learn new skills that go beyond their current understanding. They need to be willing to have an open mind in the sense that one has to learn theories that are very complex, abstract, and difficult to understand but at the same time be good at figuring out what professors want to see on exams and giving back that information. Managing this is not easy.

For my physics students, this is often centered around mathematics. This is similar to a chemistry or engineering major. Applying this to writing, reading, and reason, will likely make you a strong political science, philosophy, or nursing major. Mathematics is a challenge for many students, and it shows up in how hard a major might be. Chemistry and neuroscience might seem harder than business and political science. But all of these majors can be hard. Consider that about 40% of college students don't make it to graduation!

Often times people will talk about something called a growth mindset. This can be roughly defined as an ability that someone has that will enable them to overcome obstacles through curiosity and learning about problems that arise. When trying to do something, people who have a growth mindset can acknowledge that learning is not simple and that one has to be poor at something before they can become experts. In the long run, having a growth mindset is crucial for achieving success. I hate it when people take the next step and say, *it's so easy, just have a growth mindset and everything will be fine.* Now, in addition to stressing about your grades, it's time to stress about whether your mindset is sufficiently growth-orientated. But having the right mindset is critical for success.

But having a growth mindset and learning how to deal with setbacks may not be enough. There also needs to be a certain amount of flare and confidence associated with being successful. Often times these types of things you have when people are already experts at a particular topic. They may say that they are in college to learn, but in reality, they are in college to dominate with already developed skills from a strong high school experience. These are people who have confidence from being intelligent and demonstrate the ability of knowing things in a nonchalant manner without having to study. The trick for success is that you need to be able to channel both the growth mindset (that's the ability to overcome problems) while simultaneously being able to display confidence and the ability that you're able to accomplish things in a deep manner. And let's face it, you have to do all of this in less than a semester. It may feel as if you've gotta be everything to everybody all the time and there is no doubt that that is an oxymoron. You may find that it feels almost impossible to accomplish. And to make matters worse, there are some people who actually seem to pull it off.

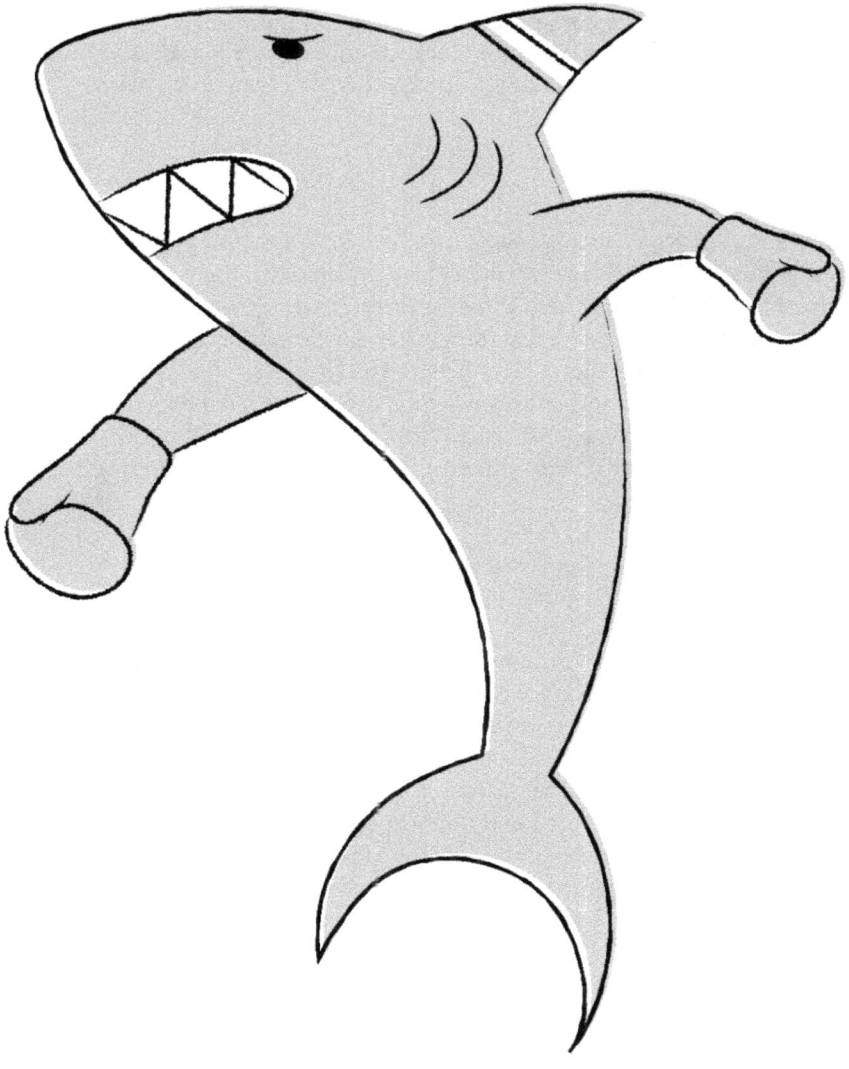

So, what do you do? It's not enough to just have a growth mindset. Yes, we need to be continually learning. But we also need something more. We need to have confidence. We need to be a little stubborn. We need to be proactive and hungry (like sharks looking for our next meal). And, like it or not, we may need to do it with a smile and likely on a team. We recommend updating our idea of the growth mindset for success in 2025 and beyond. In other words, we need to **Be a Shark!**

In the following pages, you'll learn about the shark mindset. This mindset will give you the tools and most importantly the confidence to excel and share your strengths with the community. It will give you the ability to overcome what people see as major obstacles while simultaneously giving the people around you the confidence that you are the one who can do it. We say, Be a Shark, and we mean it!

A. Problems we are facing

My wife says that you all know what the American Dream is and I shouldn't take the time to introduce it to you. The problem with the American Dream is that it isn't well defined, and it means different things to different people. So, I thought I would take a few minutes and define it, because I think it is important to think through. "The American Dream" is an idea that is continuously evolving and somehow always paramount in news talk shows your parents are watching. An article from the George W. Bush Institute titled, "A Brief History of the American Dream" by Sarah Churchwell says of the American dream:

> If you ask most people around the world what they mean by the "American dream," nearly all will respond with some version of upward social mobility, the American success story, or the self-made man (rarely the self-made woman). Perhaps they will invoke the symbolic house with a white picket fence that suggests economic self-sufficiency and security; many will associate the phrase with the land of opportunity for immigrants. No less an authority than the Oxford English Dictionary defines the American dream as "the ideal that every citizen of the United States should have an equal opportunity to achieve success and prosperity through hard work, determination, and initiative."

Is the American dream alive today? At first you might think that the answer is no. This is especially true when you read article titles like "American Dream collapsing for young adults, study says, as odds plunge that children will earn more than their parents" in the Washington Post and "U.S. Kids Now Less Likely to Earn More Than Their Parents" in NPR (National Public Radio).

But also consider the following new companies: Amazon, Visa, UnitedHealth Group, Microsoft, and Apple – which are all major companies with household names. All are relatively new companies and have made plenty of millionaires among them. Consider the following. I am writing this book for college students. I am only 49 years old. As a 19-year-old who used the internet for the first time in college, I did not use Google - it didn't even exist - it started in 1998. I am literally older than Google. However, let me ask you this. In their short lives, how much has Google, Amazon, or UnitedHealth Group changed society? Our society is changing so fast it is hard to keep up – even if day-to-day things look like they are moving slow.

For better or worse, there seems to be limited opportunity for the hardworking average Joe who doesn't apply himself. On the other hand, for the folks that want to be bold and make change, there do seem to be ample opportunities for success. How do you navigate all of that? Especially, in a winner-take all world where more and more wealth ends up in the hands of the few. The gist: opportunities are there, you just got to fight for them.

The topic of this book is **YOU** and how much of a badass you are. You too can be a shark! We are going to answer the following question, how do you do well for yourself in our current state of capitalism? Of course, it would be nice to fix all the world's problems. And I hope you or one of the readers of this book can solve them. But until that happens, we have to live in the society we have. This is a guidebook for how to achieve that success. Be a shark bitches!

Toward this end, I want to dive into the minutiae of an old idea that aligns with the American experience. The phrase is "go west young man". The general idea of this stems from early America: when you found your prospects limited, such as in a highly-populated east coast city, you could have packed your bags and searched for opportunity in a more western city/region where "society" had not "developed" as much as it had on the east coast. There you could start over and make success for yourself and innovate. So, you would give this advice to a young lad who wanted to make a name for themselves but was struggling. Can you go west? Your "D" in your Freshman English class seriously hurts your prospects of going to medical school. Or maybe it is even the controversial YouTube video you made when you were 15? Where is the west, when everywhere on the globe is occupied and watched from satellite?

The west does exist! We are making it in outer space, the ocean, new technologies, and the metaverse. Every new discovery opens up a NEW west — your west.

There is a better world out there. We have to make it happen, with compassion, and we must find a way to live in equilibrium. This is something that we need to think about and actively act on as we rise. But if we dwell on all the bad, how will we ever push ourselves forward? We need to dream big! Work hard! Practice our skills! And put ourselves into situations where we can be successful. Be an effing shark. Find and take your next opportunity.

2 WHY SHARKS?

As I talk about the shark mindset to folks, I get two very different and interesting responses. Many times, I get "Sharks! That's so badass!" The other response is why sharks – they are so mean and aggressive?

There are good reasons why we chose the shark. I'm going share some of those details in this chapter and try to hone in on what the mindset is.

A. Shark Tank

Shark Tank is one of the more successful non-fiction TV shows out there. Shark Tank aired from 2009 to the present and was put together by ABC. Most of the people reading this book are at least somewhat familiar with how the Shark Tank TV show goes, but I'm going to give you a little bit of a recap just to guide our conversation.

Shark Tank consists of two different groups. The first group, the sharks, is about five or so pseudo-venture capitalists who are looking to invest in small businesses. Like most venture capitalists they want to invest and make a shit-ton of money. But it's not just about investing the money into the business, it's also about the process and the management of the startup company. So, if they make a deal, these people go in and add value by providing their leadership skills, which adds an additional level to the money that they are provided. Of course, the ultimate aim is for them to get a huge return on investment and make a lot of money off the process.

The second group that is involved in Shark Tank is the entrepreneurs. These are people who have started a small business, started making money, and are looking to grow their business from some small-time thing to something that has a national or international presence. So, they're seeking money from the venture capitalists - the sharks - to help them grow their business. Of course, for the entrepreneurs, it's also not just about money. It's also about the professional connections and leadership that collaborating with a venture capitalist can have in their company.

The entrepreneurs come out and they provide a short 20-minute pitch of their idea, usually lots of product samples, and then the wheeling and dealing begins. The sharks try to determine whether or not they want to invest in this business and how much they would invest. They base this desire to invest on how good the idea is and how hungry the entrepreneurs are. There is an ongoing conversation between the sharks and entrepreneurs to determine if there is a possible match between the entrepreneur and one of the venture capitalists.

It's a very exciting TV show and pulls you in because it's all real and the stakes are high. As far as I know, it's not really fiction or scripted. I imagine most of the time bigger venture firms are dealing with more exotic, more expensive, and more technological pitches than what you find on this made for TV show. That said, most of the elements are there, and it gives you a glimpse of what it would be like to pitch your start-up business to investors. It also allows you to understand how you should interact and invest in your money. That it is always important to ask what kind of return am I going to get on an investment? What's the value to me as the investor? What is the risk?

And, seriously, what popular culture TV show highlights aspects of math? Shark Tank does this. And it's exciting. And it's great to see when kids take it seriously and they think about doing things like pitching their businesses that they created. Even some of the entrepreneurs who present their businesses are children. Amazing!

B. Innovation

So, whenever I start talking about "Be the Shark", folks will often say, you mean Shark Tank. Which, of course, I do, sort of, and some of the time. The show stars the "The Sharks". These are the people who are supposed to be swimming around looking for financial opportunities to attack. Basically, pouncing on young business owners who have created something special and trading their capital and experience for opportunity, and laughing all the way to the bank.

Maybe, but I tend to think about it in a different way. Both the Sharks and the entrepreneurs are thinking differently than the rest of the world. They are trying to be innovative and make meaningful change in the world – and hopefully making some money along the way.

In that sense, both groups of people who are meaningfully trying to change the world and in doing so becoming top of the food chain, are sharks. You need to be willing to accept risk, take chances, and go for success. When I talk about "aggressiveness," this is what I mean. We have to be able to work hard and take risks to be successful.

Share Resources for Success

Say what you want about capitalism, for better or worse, this is the society that we live in. I think the role of the venture capitalists encapsulates this kind of thinking, and it's something that we should embrace at least on some level in our own professional careers. Simply, when in Rome, do as the Romans do. The Romans *did* change the world.

The venture capitalist is out to make money - a lot of money! To do this, they do take on a lot of responsibility and a considerable amount of risk. They're going to invest a lot of resources into projects that they have paid to be a part of because they want it to be successful. One of those resources is likely their own time. That is going to take them away from doing other very important things. So, the way I see it is, they're leveraging the resources that they have possession of to help the entrepreneurs get their businesses off the ground. Notice I don't say money because sometimes they're not going to be investing money - we're going to have to use other resources to make things successful. Investing in ourselves is always a good plan, but it often doesn't scale as well as investing in others. When we invest in others, although we share risk, we can also share the big profits that come from working together.

By the same token, the entrepreneurs are trying to make it for themselves and they often don't have the money. They may just have the idea, which is only in the beginning of development. The infrastructure is not there for something major yet. The team is still too small. By soliciting help from sharks who have talents and resources they don't have, they can grow their idea to become something large and successful.

If one shark makes a kill and there is blood in the water, other sharks are going to come too. Everyone wins! So, when I talk about "being a shark," I am talking about something that is slightly different than Shark Tank. But it surely is related. ABC and the show runners have done such a good job of building a brand here. Let's build on top of that.

C. Sharks are the Top Predators

Sharks are at the top of the food chain! They are apex predators. There are very few creatures that keep up with them. For sure, a killer whale makes a snack of a shark from time to time, and of course, little sharks are being eaten all over the place, but for the most part, the shark is one of the most powerful predators in the ocean, and not just now but for millions of years. They are literally dinosaurs.

They were the villain in not just one movie but in a bunch of them, including the 1979 classic Jaws. So, should we strive to be the apex predators of our own communities? For sure, Mr. Wonderful – Kevin O'Leary, the very controversial shark from Shark Tank who embodies many of the negative sides of capitalism (e.g., Greed is good) – likely agrees with that. In practice, I think it is difficult to tease out that kind of thing. Of course, I feel we should be nice and community-driven. We should desire to be positively connected to our brothers and sisters in the community. We should also share with one another. However, in the professional world, it is also important to keep your eye on the prize. While we may be friendly and kind to one another, we are also fighting against one another in a giant game of king of the hill. Getting to the top may not always be a zero-sum, but it often is. Sometimes we have to protect our hunting ground and make it strong so that'll make us strong.

When someone hears this argument, they may shoot back, we all can't be sharks because then we would all be successful and rich and that isn't supported by our capitalist society. There is definitely some truth to that. I should unpack here that being a shark doesn't necessarily mean having more money. It means that you are comfortable in your environment and you're in a place where you're the one that makes the waves – and you are doing so actively - and that can be different things for different people. So, let me share with you an opportunity or a situation where I found being a shark actually had such a positive impact on my life that it absolutely changed my trajectory into radically new directions, and there was no money involved.

About the year 2000, I started to learn how to swing dance and I was pretty terrible at first. I couldn't even keep the rhythm. It was not pleasant, but it was the kind of thing where you could work hard, learn from the best and kind of make a name for yourself within this community. I'm talking a little tiny community. In the entire state of Connecticut, there were only about 100 or so "dancers" – though there were so many people who just came out now and again to dance. I got good enough where I started teaching. To be clear, I still wasn't great or anything. There were national and even international dancers who were 100s of times better than me at both dancing and teaching. But there was a time around 2006 where I had risen to a leadership role within my dance community.

I taught lessons before some of the dances, usually on the wacky side of some part of swing dancing. It felt wonderful walking into a dance and meeting up with friends. When I came there, it was as if I owned a little spot on the floor. When I walked in, everybody knew who I was, and they would stop and chat with me. People would ask each other questions and we would all get together and go out after the dance for a snack. This kind of thing gives someone confidence. As a leader in this small community, I was able to feel good about myself and believe that I can be a leader. So then, when I came back to my very competitive field of atomic physics, I believed that I could do it there too! Among our dance group, we had high school teachers and graphic designers and carpenters and professors, and the list just goes on and on. When able to connect with these people, it gave us all a feeling of being a leader in the community. Then when we had to go and interact in our very silo disciplines where the opportunities to get ahead are more cutthroat and more difficult, we were able to rely on this world that we had built for ourselves. So, by being a shark in that swing dancing community and helping my peers learn to dance, it raised me up across the board. By connecting with these people, I came away from it with a sense of leadership. I could feel that my status in the community was rising and it allowed me to be successful not just in the swing dancing community but in the other things that I tried. It gave me the confidence to believe that I am amazing and can do anything.

So, do we have to be top predators, going out and hurting people? Obviously not because that's not how society works and we don't want to be mean to one another. We want to work together. But at the same time, we also have to be looking out for our own interests. You are in control of your own life.

D. They Keep Swimming

One other really cool thing about many sharks is that they're always swimming, right? They are always moving forward to keep water (and thus oxygen) flowing into their bodies. We must also think like a shark and keep swimming.

As innovators, movers, and shakers we always have to be on the lookout for the next big idea or an interesting connection. Inspiration can be found from unexpected sources as we move through our lives. I literally keep a notebook by my bed, so that when I dream up an interesting atomic experiment, I can quickly jot it down before I lose it to the void. Some of my best ideas have come in the shower. And I can't tell you how many times I had a conversation with a family member or friend when I get an inspiration that pushes me in a new direction. Sometimes it is obvious. Sometimes it isn't. Surrounding yourself by people who think differently than you can be a successful way to generate new ideas. At a minimum, you'll have some amazing conversations with people.

The simplest example hits home for me. I am a physicist and my wife is an entrepreneur/writer. We have very different ways of thinking. Her training is in communication. However, at the same time, I have learned so much from her, that I have been able to start mixing physics and writing in interesting ways (like writing a book about being a shark). Each conversation we have gives me new insight into things I have never considered before.

Obviously, I'm not telling people they can't relax and need to be on their toes 100% of the time. I want to make a comment about this. This is something that I find to be problematic with folks, especially today. Society seems to be polarized. There are a certain number of people who are out there doing every little detail and making it perfect – often to the point where they are unhealthy because of it. They have taken the shark mindset too far. Listen if you are fighting too hard and you get injured in the wild, it's really bad for your future. Injured wild animals are very likely to die. One also needs to be aware that they can take this too far. Sometimes, when I say be a shark, they hear the message and think they need to do more. They don't. They are already a shark.

However, a large number of students who I work with do the bare minimum when they are working on projects, homework, or studying for exams. The bare minimum is not enough in a world filled with artificial intelligence. ChatGPT and others like it can already do the minimum. If all you can bring to the table is the minimum then you are not hirable. You must be able to do hard things. And the only way to get good at doing hard things is to practice doing hard things. This group has to up their game. The future is very bleak for people who are so-so workers.

E. Teeth (They are Sharp and Always Growing Back)

Be A Shark

Sharks have a lot of teeth! I love the picture of a shark, grinning with all of their rows of teeth, bearing out, looking threatening to the world. I'm looking at this picture of a shark in my living room and I am slightly scared and it's just a picture. I am nowhere near a shark right now and likely will not cross paths with one in the near future. Well except fishing, I have been lucky to see some sharks caught by others.

Sharks have rows of teeth that are strong and keep growing. It is necessary for sharks to have sharp teeth. These teeth are going to fall out because they've been used too much. But new teeth are ever ready to take their place. I think that today's young professionals need to take that analogy and go with it. They grow back for a reason.

You got to be biting the crap out of everything. If you try to get into an elite college, you have to have résumé line after résumé line of things you've tried. I imagine that what people read when they hear this is that you have to be good at everything. This is especially true for the over-involved parent who wants to make their kid the most successful kid in the world. My guess is that the college admissions advisor is not so much looking for how successful you are, but how much you're willing to put yourself out there and try to be an active member of the community. Getting to the bottom of this question: how much is this candidate contributing? They want college students who are successful for sure, but they also want college students who are connected to the school and who are going to buy into the school's mission and donate a shit-ton of money someday. They are not looking for loners who are going to stay in their dorm room and play on their computers (or equivalent) all day.

So, this has translated into an interesting development, because many high schoolers who want to go to an elite school will ask to join my research lab. Being an atomic physicist for a year or two is bound to help you get into college, right? So, each year, a bunch of students ask to join my lab. At this point I will spend some time doing some soul searching and ask myself if I have time to help. If I do, I will meet with the student and brainstorm a project for them. The students (and often their schools) are sometimes disappointed when we get started and immediately run into barriers. The high school student might say, "if I don't get a finished project, I cannot win the science competition." Which, of course, is hysterical from a professor's point of view. How can you even have a science competition? Science isn't a competition, it's about consensus through reasoning and experiment. (Though, for the record, it can feel like a competition, especially when you are in a research group trying to be the first to demonstrate a particular effect.)

Research is hard. Like really hard. Sometimes you win, sometimes you lose.

But that is ok. If you are doing hard things and trying to cut those teeth of yours, you will be amazing. The admissions folks at schools know what research is about. They know it doesn't always work out. It's not just about winning. It's about how you dealt with adversity when working on the project. These are things to write about in your essay. These are things that come out during the letter of recommendation I ultimately will write for the student, and will likely be something that comes out in their essays.

Of course, this doesn't take away from the people who win these kinds of awards. Building a community and a successful project is really hard, especially when you are in high school and have limited time to work on these projects. If this is you, keep going, you are doing great!

The most important things are: did you try (like try really hard), were you capable of finding solutions by yourself, and were you capable of finding solutions by working on a team?

The other thing is that you don't have to wait around for a big research lab to invite you to work with them. Grab a Raspberry Pi Pico, a couple of sensors, and start your own science project for less than $100. Here are some cool examples:

- Build a Raspberry Pi Pico ultrasonic sensor.
- Build a Raspberry Pi Pico infrared temperature sensor
- Build a Raspberry Pi Pico laser detector for measuring bacterial growth.

Just Google searching one of these projects is interesting and one can find step by step instructions. As you get better, the shark in you will start to see their own creative uses for this technology. A successful creative project is as good as a formal research project in a lab, if you can present it at these high-level science fairs.

E. Dinosaurs – Be Able to Adapt

Sharks have found a way to continuously adapt. As young professionals we need to continuously adapt. We need to be able to continuously do amazing things. We have to be able to keep up with a world where technology is creating and destroying businesses every day. For this final section of the chapter, I want to talk about how unsexy sharks are. They are dinosaurs, literally. Everything else went extinct. Only a handful of creatures that lived during the Jurassic age are still around today, and sharks are one of them. They have got to be doing something right, right?

Be A Shark

Typically, when students first take their introduction to physics class at college they go through projectile motion and Newton's three laws and how they're applied to get a wooden block sliding down an incline. Other down right amazing topics are why things float and how bicycle wheels roll. Not exactly the sexiest topics. However, it's easy to get your hands on these, because you can quickly build and then watch a block slide down an inclined plane. You can try out different things and see how they connect to the physics. Quickly you can start answering questions like: is your understanding better or worse? Can you predict what is going to happen? This is the way physics has been taught for a long time.

The traditional intro physics class starts off with things like blocks sliding down incline planes and projectile motion. The class ends with things like waves, springs, and wheels. Waves and springs oscillate over and over and over again. In this way, students are exposed to underlying mechanics of the universe. The wheels go round and round, right? I often tell students that the shit in nature that we really care about studying is the stuff that happens over and over and over again, because it happens over and over and over again. That makes easy to capture and connect to a model so we can make a connection between our predictions and our experiments.

This is happening all over science. For example, in chemistry you could imagine that somebody discovers molecules. Woo hoo! One of the first things the chemist might study is how the molecules vibrate and rotate. Since these properties are continually happening, they are often the first things to be mapped out. They are properties of the molecule. They are amazing to dive into because their values can literally tell you all about the molecule you just discovered.

I mean, isn't it freaking mind blowing that the Earth orbits the sun in a well-defined time? Isn't it amazing that pendulums oscillate with the same frequency each time? What about a molecule that always vibrates with the exact same frequency? There seems to be something about these processes that persists endlessly. Sharks be like that too! They're just bad ass to the maximum. They don't go away. They keep surviving basically no matter what.

Ice age?

No problem! Sharks survive!

Overheating Earth?

No problem! Sharks survive!

Stressed about your College Physics Course.

No Problem! Sharks Survive!

Sharks have found a way to continuously adapt. As young professionals we need to continuously adapt. We need to be able to continuously do amazing things and part of that is to not be bogged down with all the details.

3 IT'S MORE THAN ONE NUMBER, IT'S GRIT?

Hard work, overcoming obstacles, and building a network of people who know you, trust you, and care about you are at the core of being a shark. They pay dividends beyond what you might think. Consider the following letter of reference I wrote for a student. This student wasn't the best in the class or in the research lab. The student made a variety of mistakes, but after reading this letter, tell me you wouldn't want her on your team. Let's call her Nancy.

> To Whom It May Concern:
>
> I am honored to be writing a letter of recommendation for Nancy. I am Nancy's research advisor. She has been working in my lab since her freshman year. ... Nancy's experience in the research lab ranks high compared to everyone in terms of grit, experimental physics problem solving ability, and getting things done. The past two summers she worked in my research lab in a paid fellowship. You too will want her on your team.
>
> Nancy's skill set focuses mostly around... Entering in her junior year, I was already comfortable having her being a team leader in the lab, working on solo projects, and sending her to conferences to represent the lab.
>
> Nancy's biggest skill is her "tenacity". Usually I use the word "grit" here to describe this skill and of course that applies too. But there is a certain style to Nancy's ability to overcome obstacles in her way. She is unafraid to learn things she doesn't know. She is continuously improving.

Be A Shark

She works hard to make exciting things happen in the lab.

Nancy is an activist and environmentalist. She is the kind of person who stands up for what she believes in. She is exactly the kind of physicist we want in the 21st century. She is more than just science all of the time – she understands that our impact is much greater. She participates in ...

I was fortunate to have had Nancy in Physics for Science Majors 1; she achieved a B in the class which puts her at the 50th percentile. ... She is exactly the person they are talking about when they say it's about grit and not test taking ability. Nancy is a future star. Typically, students that come from Nancy's set of experiences would never have made it this far in physics and would have been pushed out. (Physics retention rates are poor at best.) Consider that when she came to Adelphi she was a C/B student and as a senior she was a B+/A student. While her grade point average is a 3.3, this semester she had a 3.7.

There were a number of factors that limited Nancy's success as she was a lower-level undergraduate student. Her family life was far from ideal and put her in difficult situations, e.g., she had substantial familial care responsibilities and she commuted to Adelphi by car and train during much of her time here. This trek was more than hour each way regardless of her means of travel. During one of the summers, she broke her hand in an accident. Nancy somehow always found the time to come in and work. ... It was too much and her grades suffered a bit. During her last year, she focused on school solely and her grades soared.

I believe that going to graduate school will be a fresh start for Nancy. She is hungry for the opportunity to focus on physics. Moving to a new town and not having familial obligations will give her the chance for her to focus on her studies. I see her doing what she needs to do to get through the first few years of graduate school: classes, qualifying exams, etc. Then when she gets into your lab she will be one of your top students.

Most physicist students are only limited to the technical part of science. Nancy has the ability to be successful in a range of careers including science policy or science research.

...

> We need people like Nancy in the upper echelons of physics. I am proud to be Nancy's mentor. I strongly recommend that you accept her into your program. Please let me know if you have any further follow-up questions about Nancy.

Notice that she has a 3.3 student in physics. This is a good solid GPA. And I am proud of her. However, when one considers that the average GPA at Adelphi according to a Google search is a 3.69. This puts things into context. This is a below average student, but I am willing to fully endorse her as one of my best students because she was a shark.

The GPA isn't as important as people think. As with all metrics you should strive to optimize it. However, there are other metrics at play here. And it is important to optimize those as well. The best way to do that is to be a shark.

I remember this brash first-year college student. I knew his family and had worked with one of his family members before to great success. So, in addition to the fact that I care about all of the students that walk through my door, there was a little extra love for this student. I wanted him to be successful. Like many first-year students in the physical sciences, it was not happening. Let's call him Jorge, and Jorge got off to a shitty start in college.

Calculus I or Physics I is a very difficult class for many college students. For many it is when they have to first think abstractly about open-ended problems, as high school can often be about filling out multiple choice exams. In a multiple-choice question, the answer is right in front of you. The difficulty is in selecting which one is correct. Many people are great at wading through the options and picking the correct answer most of the time. However, in Calculus I it can be the first time that someone has to contend with a question where they have to supply all of the information to solve the problem. These "short response" or even "long response" problems can be difficult to answer. There are no hints. You do or you don't. So many scared students hand in exams that are completely blank – as their teacher this really hurts.

This explains why so many students end up with Ds and Fs in this class. The struggle is real. In my physics classes, it is not unusual for students to run out of the room mid test crying. Obviously as the instructor, I know this is a problem and work hard to prepare students for this moment. However, if a student isn't prepared, isn't paying attention or isn't trying (assuming they can figure it out on test day just like they did in their high school classes), it can often cause problems. If a student isn't prepared to take the exam, it can be overwhelming for them. So often, I run across students who are not prepared and bomb-hard!

Jorge did bomb and it was painful. After the semester, there was the usual talk about how he might choose another major in school. This can be a good decision of course. If a student is struggling because they hate doing math, then they should get out of physics. However, I find that it is often a situation where the student is looking for an easy out. Sure, college may be easier if you choose a different major. However, at some point in your career, you are going to be asked to deliver when the shit is hitting the fan. I find that if you know yourself better, it is easier to make it all happen.

So, Jorge came to the faculty and said I want to be a good student. And then asked how to do it? We gave the usual answer, which step-by-step tells a student how they can go from failure to success. Most people don't do it because it is hard. Jorge did it. The problem isn't usually how to do it. The problem is usually having the "will" to do it.

Jorge first crawled, then walked, and by the time he was a senior, he was running. It was actually quite beautiful. He left our school as one of the best students and entered into an amazing Ph.D. program.

The point is, it wasn't easy. Mistakes we make when we are young can have lasting effects. I vividly remember cringing when Jorge got his grades as a senior. Despite getting straight As, his GPA was still low from his first-year courses that he failed. And he had to own up to this when he applied to graduate school. This student was 100% shark!

It has been my experience, that young people in school think they have to be perfect to get ahead. If their GPA isn't 3.8 or a 4.0 then they can't be successful. And in some cases, this is in fact true. But it has been my experience that if you show that you can overcome major obstacles, there are going to be people who are going to see your growth and they are going to want you on their team. If you are doing routine medical surgeries, you might want a straight A student who is perfect. But if you want someone who can be innovative and entrepreneurial, you are going to want someone who can overcome obstacles – because, and I tell you from firsthand experience, being on a state-of-the-art research project is about solving one major obstacle after another. It is both the best ride ever and **it blows donkey chunks**.

People who know, know. And they are looking for sharks. So, what you might see as a huge negative, can be a huge win. It's not just about spinning a bad situation to look like a good one, it's about demonstrating how to overcome obstacles. Jorge's cumulative GPA was a little lower than you might think because of his poor first year of school. Never mind that, his college career was a complete success. Jorge showed us what it takes to win. You have to be willing and able to overcome major obstacles in your path toward success. You cannot be idle. Be a shark, just like Jorge.

You might ask what is the step-by-step process we gave Jorge. Here are the things we recommended.

- Read textbook, filling in missing steps, for the associated chapters
- Know how to do all of the homework problems (without having to look up answers at all)
- Do a practice exam after studying a bit in game-like conditions a couple of days before the exam.
- Know how to do all of the in-class problems *without* having to look up answers before the exam.
- After studying for a while, make a list of all of the things that you do not know. Then go learn what is on your list.
- Reach out to a subject matter expert and discuss things you did not know: professor's office hours, upper-classmen, even friends.
- Build a team from the class to check-in and work with them but be careful. Be careful, do not let other people do the work for you, but rather work with them in a team together.

4 HUSTLING IN COLLEGE

One of my favorite Internet personalities is Gary Vee (Gary Vaynerchuk). He's funny! He's energetic! He's positive! He's empathetic! He makes you feel like he knows what the secret sauce is and he knows how to teach it to you to make your life wonderful. I actually watch this guy a lot to try to figure out how to connect to my students better. This guy is the man! He knows how to talk to people. And I agree with him almost all of the time. I strongly encourage you to open up TikTok or some other social media app and search him up. He is an interesting dude.

Gary Vee is part of a culture called hustle porn - man I hate that name. But the gist of what his argument is and others like him is: why should you be spending time going to college and wasting your money on stuff that doesn't really matter, when you can be working towards success in life? Answer: all you have to do is hustle. Or in other words, pick an idea, such as starting a business or becoming a social media influencer, and then work very hard to make that a reality. Be tireless! Learn from your mistakes! And constantly grow.

There are a lot of really good things in there. Hustle is amazing and it's something that you should have professionally no matter what you do. You do need to push yourself hard and hustle through issues that arise. You need to make your own destiny, and all of the stuff that Vee says on this front is 100% true!

The devil is in the details. Let's break it down.

One of the things that these hustle porn leaders push for is the idea that hard work is the key. As if somebody could be successful through hard work only. Isn't that the American dream? If you just work harder, success will happen.

It's not just hard work that leads to success. I strongly encourage you to take a field trip to your local McDonald's (or equivalent) at lunchtime this afternoon. When you go inside and place your order, look in the back at the people who are working. They are running around with their heads cut off, working as hard as you could ever possibly see. It blows my mind how hard fast-food workers work, especially during rush-hour, and how little praise this hard work gets in the popular media. They work hard. And it doesn't matter how good they flip those burgers, they're never going to become the CEO - unless they push themselves beyond the typical person in intellectual prowess, creativity, etc., etc. There are multiple glass ceilings that will prevent this worker from reaching the highest heights in the corporation.

So, in addition to hard work and how hard you hustle we have to look at two separate things: **skills and opportunity**. To be an elite, you need hustle but you also need plenty of skills and even more opportunity.

One of the things that Gary Vee talks about in a lot of his speeches is that the Internet provides a pathway to success that a generation ago was impossible. It is possible for somebody to sit down, create some TikToks or YouTube videos and turn whatever idea they have into gold. So, with some creativity, hard work, and a little luck you too can be a billionaire. And this has been a pathway to success for many people.

Is it possible for somebody to get out there and do all of these things to create a successful business without going to college? Yes! If you are interested, should you try it? Yes! Go for it! Especially when you are young, without the burden of family and children. In high school, I played baseball in the hopes of being a professional baseball player. Was it ever going to happen? Nope! Did I gain a lot by trying to do it? YES! Same thing goes with starting a rock band. Do it, if nothing else it will be fun and possibly a way to make lifelong friends. Of course, it is the growth mindset, the process of trying and actually learning things that makes someone successful in the long term. Working hard and learning is always a good idea.

But the odds aren't in your favor. It's hard to make it from scratch. And a lot of successful people out there who seem like they are starting from scratch aren't. Consider that President Donald Trump styles himself as a self-made businessman. His dad only gave him a million dollars to get started. That is opportunity that almost nobody in the world actually has. It's not just money. A lot of the would-be pop stars start out as child stars. Consider Justin Timberlake and Britney Spears were both child cast members on the Disney Channel variety show The All-New Mickey Mouse Club. Still, they would not have made it if they didn't work hard and have good ideas. It's a tough world out there, even for the rich and famous. Everyone is hustling, but that is not enough.

According to the hustle porn propaganda, all of these really good ideas about hustling and working hard to make your dreams come true are inconsistent with going to college. There's an idea out there that going to college is in the exact opposite vain than what the hustle porn folks are saying. Don't go to college–just hustle and work hard– is kind of the message that is leading through our society and social media. I promise you that if you hustle in my physics class, it will lead to great things in life. Highly educated people who hustle are in high demand.

So, every teacher, advisor and parent are telling us go to college, go to college, go to college. And Gary Vee is saying, don't go to college, just work hard on the things that you care about and be really crafty about them and you'll make a career out of them. Who is right?

That is an interesting question! 40% of students who attend college don't get their degree, college retention rates are about 60%. Let me say that one again for everybody in the back. About 40% of college students don't graduate, and for them Vee is 100% correct. If you're among the 40%, why waste your time in college trying to get a degree which you won't get? You won't see the benefits of your time in school or money spent. For you, you could spend your time hustling and turning a business into success - which can give you real returns and not end up losing money via student loans. This is a no-brainer. I don't know why we're not talking about this more in society. 40% of college students don't make it after six years of school at their college!

With 40% of college students not making it through college, you might imagine that professors are in a kind of gang where we dress up in street clothes and baseball bats and go around and find students to knock on the head and take their money – "Give me all ya got bitches" like we are some kind of evil gang whose goal in life is to destroy students and their prospects for success. This opinion may be the view that Fox News has for college professors these days, but reality is so much different. As a body, many of us are distraught because we want to see our students be successful and we're often just asking for the bare minimum. We are doing everything we can to help you. If you try a little at your work and do reasonably close to the best you can you are going to be okay – even if you slip up. Almost every situation being okay is enough to get a C in the class, if not an A. Remember the average GPA is like a 3.6. In almost every case, professors (that I know) want their students to be successful in life and want to do everything they can do to help. We view ourselves as shark trainers.

So, among students, I see this really interesting dichotomy. They say things like, "Gary Vee says I should drop out of school, start a business, and start hustling. Failing out of school isn't going to help me." Yes, but if that same student would spend a little bit of time on their homework set then they would get a reasonable grade in my class. That reasonable effort will lead to a degree. Participating in the system also creates opportunity. Why don't these folks hustle in their pursuit of their degree? I have never failed anyone for not being smart enough. But I fail people for not trying – seriously all the time. That's the thing, Gary Vee's advice on hustling is actually great advice, but somewhere and somehow the students think that we're not talking about hustling in the actual things that you are doing - like not just your job but the other avenues of life such as like dealing with your parents, being successful in school, and relationships. Because you have to work at those walks of life as well.

The big thing that I want to talk a little bit about is opportunity. If you're not connected, you're probably not going to be successful, no matter how hard you work. Does TikTok and other social media outlets provide opportunities for you to make it without going through the system? Yes, and this is one of the amazing things about these apps. But there are hidden things in those apps that aren't being discussed, at least not amongst the Gary Vees of the world, that are preventing opportunity for a lot of people. For example, the algorithms show that they want to see a rich clean house in the background and that they're going to favor somebody who gives a presentation from that point of view. The apps introduce bias that you're not even aware of. So yes, you can still overcome it by being brilliant or by sheer luck. Most people aren't going to win because just as in Blackjack it's hard to win against the house over and over again. You may win one night at the casino, but that's not going to happen if you're at the casino every single night. The deck is stacked against you, unless you have opportunity. So, you have to build opportunity and throughout this book we will tell you how.

So, it all boils down to hustle, opportunity, and skills. You can find these in colleges, and there are a number of amazing programs that can launch your career in a variety of amazing ways. For example, choosing a very career-focused major such as nursing is an excellent way to go. But so are the liberal arts – but only if you hustle. I always tell students that I don't care about your grade. My goal is to prepare you to be successful at 40 years old. While that means drastically different things for different people who all choose different careers, the focus on critical thinking, persistence when faced with challenges, being able to quickly think about a problem and get an estimate within seconds, and how learning can be fun are the metrics that I am trying to optimize. The people who take away these messages from my class, no matter what career path they take, will have the ability to be successful and know how to achieve it.

Not everyone will of course. Life is complicated. And not every professor is trying to do this in their class. There are bad professors out there for sure. Some might even be trying to indoctrinate their students with ultra-liberal ideas – none of the professors I know, though. Some, especially adjuncts, are so overworked and underpaid that it is hard to accomplish what they really want to. And some faculty are just bad. But what I have found is that most faculty really care about their students and want them to have success. And are trying really hard in the amount of time they have to make it happen. It is really up to the students to make it happen.

So, is Gary Vee and his ilk, right? Yes! You have to hustle. But there is more to the story. The fact is, unless you are coming from an ultra-wealthy family, you are also going to need opportunity and skill to make it in the world. Hustling in a well-connected world of higher education is a way for someone to gain the opportunities and skills needed to be successful.

Lets da-nah da-nah da-nah be a shark and eat the shit out of the remaining pages of this book.

Be A Shark

PART TWO:
SKILLS A SHARK WOULD HAVE

5 MASTERING SHARKYNESS!

How do I take my sharkiness to the next level? In this chapter, you'll get some key advice and dive into what it means to BE A SHARK!

Don't sweat the mistakes, keep attacking

Be innovative! But also keep in mind that when you are, you will be taking risks. And whenever you take risks, things aren't always going to go well. You will make mistakes. That is okay, when you do hard things, you will make mistakes. Learn from your mistakes and move on.

This is why the grading system in the USA makes me so upset. As start at 90, Bs start at 80, Cs at 70 and so on. And these scores can even be higher. I have seen teachers make an A start at 95%.

If an exam is so easy that you can get a 95% on it in a very short period of time say the 45 minutes of a typical high school class, then it is not really challenging you. It is testing how well you recall information or maybe how well you can perform with simple tasks. Obviously, this was a very important thing before the information age. At that time, being able to understand and access a lot of correct information on a particular topic was a necessity. However, when entire libraries of information are literally a Siri or Alexa question away, does it really matter how much information we have memorized? Of course, this is a bit of a trick. Even though all of human knowledge is a few keystrokes away, understanding that information and what to do with it in a reasonable amount of time does take a considerable amount of education. Still, if you don't remember the fourth digit in pi - it's going to be okay. It will only take a moment to look it up. Fifty years ago, this might have been different. Where is my copy of the CRC, Handbook of Chemistry and Physics when you need it? If you want to see what us dinosaurs used back in the day, Google "Handbook of Chemistry and Physics". It was a massive book filled with nothing but tables of data.

So, what does matter? I believe that what is really important to a shark is the ability to take the information out there and apply it to really hard, sick problems. Training our mind on how to be able to sort through this information is tricky, especially in a short amount of time.

I and most physicists out there typically give students really hard problems where the average score is significantly less than 85% of the standard class. Average grades on my test typically run around 55%. And if you are getting 55% of the points on this exam you are doing well and making sense of the problems. That's a B!

This can be a nightmare as an instructor, when you have a class full of pre-meds. Many of these students want to be doctors, have not gotten below a 92 on an exam ever – in some cases I actually mean forever. And they believe – somewhat mistakenly and somewhat true – that their string of As from when they were 5 years old is going to be a key thing for getting them into medical school. And then they take my exam and get a 58. A 58! They don't even know how to process it. Some people get really sad and come to my office and cry. Some people get really angry. And they come to my office and ruffle a feather or two. Either way, I appreciate when students show their emotion (within reason) because it starts an important conversation about learning and the growth mindset.

Me: "A 58! That is solid B work. Great job."

Them: "You don't know how hard I studied for this exam? Or even how many times I read the book. None of the problems in the book were on the test. In fact, I have never seen these problems before." And then it comes. As a Gen-Xer I can't even believe the words were spoken out loud. "And I deserve an A, can you change my grade?" For someone of my generation, that is as bad as waking up to your mom and calling her a "F-ing bitch". Of course, people do that today too.

Me: "No unfortunately I cannot change the grade, but I can tell you how to be successful for future exams. Would you like to work with me on that?"

The troubling point is that this student has never really had to contend with a really difficult, meaty, mind-numbing problem – in school anyway. And the first time they do, are they going to be able to deal with it? Maybe. But as these are skills – like playing the trombone – the only way you get good at it is if you practice, practice, and practice.

Consider playing a musical instrument. Reading a textbook is helpful. Reading other books on how to play is also helpful. Watching YouTube videos teaching you how to play is helpful as well – and these days YouTube is literally the one stop shop for just about anything you want to learn. But – and this is most important – consuming the information doesn't mean you have learned it. To learn it you have to try a bunch of times and fail. The failing is the critical point. If you are playing a song you want to learn how to play, and you hear the noise from the instrument doesn't match what you would expect, then you have to adjust in real time what you are doing to make those sounds. This iterative process allows you to hone in on getting the right sounds from the instrument.

This is true in your classes as well – especially when your professor gives you problems you have never seen before and you are unable to memorize a solution to a particular problem. In my opinion, I think each professor should be doing this across the university. However, I can only speak for my exams.

There are a host of reasons why physicists are making changes to this system – including trying to increase student confidence. And I have definitely added my own opinion to the conversation in the past. However, I am hoping in the future we still give the students meaty problems where they have to figure out how to solve it on the fly and they need to prepare by first failing over and over until they converge to the solution.

It is important that schools, especially colleges and universities, are a place where students have an opportunity to challenge one's self and explore what they know, what they can figure out, and what they don't know. As professionals, we are going to be challenged with difficult scenarios all of the time where there isn't a perfectly laid out procedure. To my pre-meds, I will often ask about being in the emergency room with a person with blood pouring out of their chest. You have a few moments to solve this impossible problem and it is up to you. If you are not a good problem solver, this scenario is likely to end badly for everyone involved. Still, I get pre-meds that say, we memorize everything in Biology and what you do isn't fair.

The example about failure that is often given is that it took Thomas Edison multiple failed attempts to get the light bulb working. He had to be okay with failing over and over. And while failing, he had to have the desire to learn from his mistakes. He had to keep digging to figure out what the missing pieces were on the project he was working on. Sharks do this with everything they learn – and it never stops. Sharks are always learning, innovating, failing, and rebuilding.

So, what does a shark do? We have to be continually failing toward our own version of success. We have to keep attacking from new angles until we get it right and end up with a tasty meal. Be a shark!

A. Be Thorough

Learning science is interesting. You are never really done. You are always diving in deeper and trying to make sense of things. Sometimes all of the difficult things work out perfectly. Sometimes when you dive into something it turns out to be messier than you thought and uncovers something new about how the universe works.

Be A Shark

Good enough works sometimes but it doesn't work all of the time. When you don't understand something, dive in until you understand every little detail. And of course you can't always do this, but I do try to do this as much as possible.

This happened in my research project recently. When I was analyzing data from a recent experiment, I had noticed that there was some unexpected wiggling in the data. At first, I chalked it up to noise and continued my analysis. However, as I continued to take data on this topic, I kept diving deeper. Eventually I found out that the wiggle was actually not noise and was something that was part of my data. I had to dig through a variety of different proposed theories to see if any of them explained my unexpected wiggles in the data. And then I had to learn about unexpected science as I dove deeper into understanding what was happening with the experiment.

This is how scientists think and process these kinds of events. Important things keep coming up and nagging you. Even when you think you understand something deeply, it is important to continually be testing what you know and what you don't know. Most of the time it works fine. Other times it doesn't. The important thing is that when we don't understand something, we have to dive in deeper until we do. So as a student how does this play out for you?

I remember this situation where a student came to office hours and asked for help on their homework.

Me: "Thanks for coming in today, how can I help?"

Student: "I was reading the book, I have questions, can you help me out?"

Me: "Sure"

The student opens the book to approximately the correct page only toward the end of chapter, let's say page 68. Looking over their shoulder, I am thinking this is a good page to study because there is a problem on the test taken from the material related to what is found on this page. But the student shuffles through the pages to get to page 63.

Student: "Can you explain what is happening here"

Me: "Yes ..."

Student: "That is exactly what I was thinking. And how about here:"

Be A Shark

Me... "Yes. ..."

Student: "Thank you, looks like I got the problem on the practice test 100% correct."

Me: "If you already knew it, why did you ask?"

Students: "I just wanted to make sure I got it 100% correct."

We quietly sat there for a few moments. Then:

Me: "You had started at page 68, does the material we covered on that page make sense, too?"

Student: "No"

Me: Knowing that this is the topic of the next test, "Oh, did you want to discuss it?"

Student: "No I don't understand it all."

Me: "huh?"

Student: Blinks a few times. "I don't understand it, why should I study it?"

Literally steam is bursting out of my ears like an old cartoon. This student felt it made sense to learn something if they could get everything right and understand it perfectly. The messy, difficult details on the problem they didn't understand were just deemed unimportant, because the student was so confused they couldn't even attempt to learn.

Of course, some of this was strategy. If you have a test in a few hours, you can only learn a finite amount of stuff. Better to focus on what is going to give you the greatest number of points on the exam. But in this example case, the student had a number of days for the exam, so they had plenty of time to review it.

You cannot be afraid to take on different problems and topics. When you do get confronted with something difficult, you have to make sure you are thoroughly going through the problem and trying to understand as much of the project as possible. You have to catch every detail and see how it all connects with your understanding of a situation, because details matter. Sharks face the difficulties.

Be A Shark

6 NETWORKING

A. Shark Love: Don't Over Think Networking.

When I was in college, I was lucky enough to have won a summer fellowship to do research over the summer. It was called an REU, Research Experience for Undergraduates. If you are a sophomore or junior science major you should drop everything and apply to these right now. These summer fellowships are amazing! You get paid to do science. You get to network with people in graduate school and get something amazing on your resume. As part of the summer fellowship, we were given on-campus housing. It was a nice dorm hall with about 50 rooms on three floors. On the ground floor was a common room and kitchen. At our university there were only ten or so fellows that lived in the hall. The only down side was that we were on our own for food and we all had to share the kitchen.

I immediately entered into a pack with a few other guys. Each one of us would handle dinner and dishes one night a week. So, we were only responsible for working in the kitchen one night a week and on the weekends. It was a great deal for everyone involved. One of my friends in the pack and I still laugh about the momma meatballs I made when we see each other. During that summer, everyone in the house became friends. There was the usual drama with a number of college students living in a dorm. On the whole it was a very positive summer.

Most of the relationships fizzled out and we all went our separate ways after that summer. However, a bunch of us meet up at the APS's (American Physical Society) yearly meeting. I remember walking around the conference site talking with my friend about how he wanted to ask a young woman on a date.

I was like, "dude, you should go for it." Go! Go! Go! Like any good friend would do. And he did. I believe they went on their first date at that conference.

As happens with so many people, we went our separate ways and we lost touch. However, and this is the important part, so listen closely. In my 30s I was looking for a job. I went on a job interview at a very nice place. The first person to interview me was my friend from that summer. Later on, one of the other employees took me out to lunch. She was my friend from that summer that my other friend had asked out. Are you keeping up? They did in fact go on that date at the conference and many more. In fact, they were now married. Both were working for the company I was applying for. Did I get the job offer? Yes. And I likely needed their help in the smoked-filled rooms behind the scenes. While I was successful and in my 30s, I was changing careers and didn't yet know how to present myself in this new industry. I definitely didn't have my shit together at the time. Hindsight is 20/20 yo!

I often like telling a story about love when I give my presentation on Be A Shark because I think it lowers the bar a little. When people talk about networking, it is always kind of scary. It's like you are speed dating and you have to look and act amazing or else you won't be noticed. The thing is you don't need to be any of that. You just need to be you, have fun with friends, and be positive. Later in life these connections will help you, in ways you can't even fathom.

Being a shark is not about being an asshole. It is in fact the reverse of that. It is about being hard-working, intentional, aggressive, and friendly.

It can also hinder you if you are not positive in your relationships. That doesn't mean you have to say yes to every request or be perfect all of the time. But when you say no or walk away from a job/school/group etc., do so in a friendly way. People often make decisions with information that you don't always know about. Once you get through the interview stage, jobs will literally reach out to people who know you and ask for all of the gossip. Formally it can be called reaching out to an "off-list reference". So, it pays to have a friendly attitude. Who knows what someone will say about you? And of course, that is completely out of your control. But I find that if I am nice to folks, it adds up in the end, and there's really nothing to worry about.

There are many things about the time I applied for this job in 2008 that I regret. I hadn't done my research on the company. I should have expected my friends to be a part of the interview because I should have known they worked there. I didn't. I should have done a better job of preparing for that interview. In the pages of this book, I am going to share with you many lessons that I learned the hard way. We have to do as best as we can to be a shark but also no one is perfect. Let's go ahead and drop any idea you might have that when I say be a shark, I might mean, "be an asshole" or "be mean". Apex predators like the shark still have to live with others in their environment.

B. Put yourself out there all of the time

Networking is both incredibly hard and incredibly easy. Let's first talk about how hard it is.

Why is Networking so Hard?

Public speaking is one of the hardest things many people can do. Many people would rather go to the dentist than do an event where they have to speak in public. From the outside, I imagine that networking is like public speaking. Someone might conjure up a picture of a room filled with very important people and you don't know a single one of them, and somehow are supposed to walk up to each of them, armed only with elegance and grace, and tell them why they need to hire you for double your current salary. And to make matters worse, the people not only don't want to talk to you, they hate you and want to make your life a living hell. That is exactly how I feel when someone says network. Talk about high stakes.

Sometimes it be like that though. There is nothing worse than walking into a room and you realize that you are the only person in the room that looks like you (or has the same background) and you don't know anyone in there. That's a tough one. I always struggle with that situation. Be patient with yourself. Set a reasonable goal for the amount of time you are willing to connect with people. Give it everything you have. Be nice. Smile. And as soon as you hit your target, get the hell out of the room, buy yourself some chicken wingers and head up to your hotel room for a movie – if that is your thing. (Now that I am old, I tend to avoid anything that upsets my stomach when I travel to conferences.)

Another problem is on the opposite end of the spectrum. You might know everyone in the room, but no one in the room actually knows about the thing that you want to do and network about. Well, maybe there is one person out there, but having to sift through everyone is going to take a lot of time. That is also a difficult situation.

And, what do you say when you walk up to the people? We often hear about the elevator pitch. This is a five-sentence pitch that we can give to someone. The general idea is that if you are in an elevator with someone important such as Stephen Wolfram (founder of Mathematica – hence https://www.wolframalpha.com/) you have the time until the doors open again to convince the VIP to take notice of you. What, I have to get someone famous to notice me after just a few minutes? Ah. What. eh? *Ding!* Times up. The door is opening and you missed your opportunity to ask Stephen Wolfram for an internship. Basically, networking sucks, right?

Networking is Actually Pretty Easy

Here are some pointers to make networking easy (or at least doable).

1. Follow the Golden Rule – Do unto others and you want them to do unto you. Be friendly and carry a smile unless something really bad is happening – and if so, try not to network, go punch a pillow or something. When someone asks you for help, help them if possible. A big part of networking is that people help the people they like. And connections come from strange sources. If someone asks you for homework help in a class and you say no, they are not going to introduce you to their uncle who just happens to be Stephen Wolfram.

2. Write a simple elevator speech and practice in the mirror to the point that you can give it without thinking. Here is a simple structure for one.

   <u>Who and where you are:</u> *My name is Dom Stevens and I am a junior physics major at the University of RC.*

   <u>What you are working on:</u> *I am working in Professor Wright's quantum research lab where I am exploring atomic excitation with lasers.*

   <u>Where do you want to go:</u> *I am looking to build a career in quantum physics and I am looking for opportunities that can further this career goal.*

   The more details you have, the more intense this elevator pitch can be. But I also think that a cool and calm elevator pitch is better than one that is overly intense. Too much intensity can be off putting.

   How does someone get started: Getting a chance to build a career at a company like Wolfram would be amazing. (You are not done when you get to the fourth part, this is where you turn the situation around and back to the person you are talking to. Make it a conversation.)

   Finally pivot: Preparing for the last part is difficult. I might practice with friends where your friend is play acting the person. Just so you can try out different lines. What you don't want to do is ask directly for an internship or a job.

   It is much better to ask someone a question like "What is it like working at Brookhaven National Lab? How do you get a foot in the door?" versus "Do you have any internships available?" While they may have internships and they might tell you how to apply for them, what you want to do is to build a network. Talking to the internship coordinator before you apply and building a positive relationship with them is likely going to be more successful than just getting the URL for the application. And they will likely give you that information anyways.

3. Just have fun and make friends. Really? What? Networking works when you are enjoying life and making connections with the people around you.

Separate the job search from networking. Just try to connect with as many people as possible in a positive way – when appropriate. Be nice to people. Discuss what you are working on. You are a shark; you are going to be working on amazing things. You will quickly have great things to talk about. Try to think about making new friends.

Separate doesn't mean isolated. Once you have a large group of people that you know, don't be afraid to ask people in your network directly for help. Something like "Dear so and so, I would like to get a job at company x or similar. Who do you think is the best person to talk to, to learn more about getting into this industry?"

Keep being nice to people and keep following through until doors start opening. They will open up.

Tools such as LinkedIn are amazing ways of keeping track of everyone – and how to get in touch with them. Everyone who is going through this process needs a LinkedIn account and should monitor it closely – unless I am on vacation, I make sure to check it once a day.

Nothing has to be perfect. You just have to get out there and make connections.

C. Introvert vs Extrovert

One might think that I am only talking to the extroverts here. This is not true. While as an extrovert, I am more likely to run up to someone and introduce myself; my wife, as an introvert, is significantly better at networking than I am. She develops relationships much slower than I do. However, when she does develop those relationships, they are deeper and more meaningful than the ones I develop. People come to think of her as someone who doesn't say a lot but when she does, everyone should listen.

When you go and network, you use the tools that you are comfortable with and at the level you are comfortable at. Develop relationships at the rate you are comfortable with. It is not a race to see who can grab the most business cards. It's a race to see who can develop the best relationships for the most meaningful and successful life (and career). If you go slow and steady that is fine. It can still be wildly successful.

Let me be clear, slow and steady still means you are always working on it and always making connections even at a slow rate. If you are not there making connections, then you are not networking. So, when I think of an introvert that might have success, I think about someone who is looking to develop deep connections with people slowly. An introvert who will definitely not be successful is one who doesn't meet people and try to extend themselves.

The extroverts, keep doing what you are doing. Make friends and connections. Make sure to do the leg work and develop deep meaningful connections.

7 BITE THROUGH RED TAPE! – BE PERSISTENT

A. Your First Major Obstacle Always Hurts

Getting started on something new and amazing is really an empowering experience for someone. The entrepreneurs start by thinking about what could be and they are all full of energy. I find student projects are like this to do. Ready to take on every challenge that pops up! Inevitably, as they get going, they are going to run into obstacles and these obstacles are going to do a number of things to them. One of the first difficulties they are going to run into is getting their momentum killed. When they first started a project, they were flying along. They were very excited trying to take on the world and whatever problem they are working on. Then, all of a sudden, they have got an issue(s) where the solution isn't obvious and it's taking time and energy. Its slowing them down and making it difficult to do. The entrepreneur can seem if they have concrete in their boots. As somebody who has started 100s mini projects and had them come to this point, over and over, I can tell you it's a very tough moment to experience.

For entrepreneurs and college students alike, once you lose your momentum, it can be difficult to continue. In fact, at the beginning, innovators have to be constantly evaluating whether or not it's even worth looking into. Before the big investments and hype, they have to consider whether the cost-benefit favors continuing on with the project. So not only is it so stressful because you have to think through this big sticky problem to the once amazing idea; the team also has to be considering whether they would just rather throw the whole idea away and spend time working on other things.

If you are looking for successful strategies for making it through this phase, don't ask me. In my career, I have always found this period to be one of trial and error. I found that I had to guess a little and make some assumptions. And while I always teach students how to quickly make back-of-the-envelope calculations to see whether ideas are worth pursuing, it seems that at this phase in the project you are beyond that and you already know that it is worth pursuing. Answering questions like, is it worth YOU trying to solve this problem with the resources YOU have is always really hard. This is really tricky; you can have it go either way.

This is where it's better to be a little aggressive. I feel you have to put yourself out there and make calculated decisions as best as you can. But once you decide, then you have to throw yourself at the problem. Dive in head over heels trying to sort out all of the issues, find the problems, and innovate around them.

Once you are in, be all in. Take a bite out of the problem.

B. Red Tape is the Worst

The worst problem I find is red tape. Red tape is the amount of bureaucracy, paperwork, and other tasks that someone is getting from an organization that is preventing them from achieving their task in a timely manner. It's often redundant and often very frustrating. Sometimes this is just the necessary bureaucracy of getting going and while frustrating it is something that has to be gotten through. There are often safety or cost concerns that folks don't appreciate when they start a project and this is one way of uncovering them – going through all of this paperwork can expose an issue. However, other times it can be an active process of somebody or some part of an organization that is trying to prevent the innovative person from succeeding. If regular bureaucracy is frustrating, this is downright maddening. Trying to fight uphill against an organization that's trying to keep YOU – the innovator – down. This can really be demoralizing and hurt. And this is a way a shark can get derailed.

So, while there are some people who could only be classified as assholes, I have found that most people in the world are kind people who want to work with you. If you run across somebody who is actively working against you, it is often because the innovation you're working on will be disruptive to something important to them. They may not be incentivized to want the innovation (e.g., think about the truck driver whose job will be lost by automated driving technology). You may be thinking let's go be a shark, but they are thinking about keeping the status quo.

Be A Shark

For example, if someone's trying to fix a company's efficiency at making a widget, it could ultimately lead to the company laying off some people. This is often the issue with automation. If this is the case, then a person might run into a problem with the employees of that company because they don't want to be laid off. Obviously, this makes sense from their point of view. I find that trying to understand why they're feeling the way they're feeling is really important. We do have to think about how our innovation and how our new technology is affecting the world around us. Having good conversations about it with everyone can be a helpful experience. It can be a near impossible action in other scenarios, and talking can even hinder your progress. The one thing that I feel is important is for sharks to never lose sight of the people-part of the problems you are working on.

Red tape can come at you from many levels. And it's important to think about how these different levels of red tape can get at you and hurt your momentum. So, the first level of red tape that we all run across, I would say, is the regular paperwork that we have to do when we're trying to launch something new. If you're going to buy a building or a house, there is a crap ton of documents that need to be signed and checked by a lawyer. All of this takes time, energy, and money. But these are all necessary steps and one has to go through them in order to be successful – even if they sap your energy.

One of the real big problems with red tape is what I would call general incompetence of the world. So often times with red tape you have to get other people to help you make your project go. And the person on the other side of the counter, who's working with you may not have your level of excitement. Don't believe me? Show up at the DMV when you have to change your license from one state to another. Talk about an experience that will kill your inner shark. They're doing their job and working hard. While I might be excited about changing my license after a move, chances are the DMV worker isn't as excited. While they may take pride in their work, it's not such a big deal if one or two people have to wait those extra few minutes. It's all not that big of a deal, just that when you go there, it always seems to squash a little bit of your soul.

It's just paperwork, right? But to somebody who is barely able to write and speak, he idea of doing new paperwork is terrible. I'm always trying to read these documents to understand what they're saying and what I am getting myself into. There always seems to be some deep processing that will need to be going in my head every time I go through these documents. I'm always looking at the words, afraid that I am misunderstanding something and there will be a gotcha that will hurt in the end. I really struggle with this. Maybe it's silly, but all of this brain processing time could have been spent on more productive things and going through all of the paperwork really slows one down – especially when I speak, talk, and write like a neanderthal.

There are also situations when you are at the mercy of other people. Talk about something that is difficult for a shark to take. This is a really big problem in academics. We often rely on writing grant proposals in order to get funding to do our projects. And of course, what we do in our projects determines if we are successful. As I put together a proposal, I'm often at the mercy of the person who is reading the grant and evaluating it on the other side. Do they find what I'm doing interesting? I don't know. Even if I write the perfect proposal, they could be optimizing who they select for other reasons beyond what I know about when I'm submitting. Of course, you always have to try to figure out what they want and give it to them. But in the

Be A Shark

end, it's hard to get into their head when you don't know who the reviewer is, and you'll never know what anybody is actually thinking. So, some grant proposals win, some grant proposals lose. Actually, most grants lose but every now and then you get lucky. The hard part of grant proposals for me is while I may be able to do my part as good as possible who knows what will actually happen in the smoke-filled rooms where the decisions are made.

This thing is that when I submit my proposal it has to be submitted by the university and people that I work with have to sign off on it. They may or may not have comments. And sometimes incorporating their comments can be difficult and make slight changes to what you are doing. They can also be demoralizing when the finance at the university person yells at you for being an idiot – which happens more than I care to admit.

Consider this story, I wrote this grant proposal that I was submitting for a project that I'm working on. It wasn't perfect, but it was pretty good when I was done with it. I solicited feedback from a couple of experts and tried to incorporate their feedback as best as possible. Again, it wasn't perfect, but it was a good start. So, I am getting ready to submit this proposal to a number of different places. One of the people who is associated with this project decided that it would be best if they submitted it from their organization. As this organization was one of the best, most trustworthy organizations in the country, it sounded like an excellent idea. I worked with the team from this company to modify my grant proposal over the course of a week. It was amazing in the end. We actually strengthened the proposal a little bit; however, it was hard to get consensus in the end. We ended up missing the deadline because of all of the back and forth. So, even after we spent an entire week with a team of like four or five people, (well-paid, high-level people) we weren't able to get the proposal done on time. I was literally bashing my head against the wall because it was so bad. As we were putting it together and we got close to the deadline I would reach out to the group and was like, is everything OK? Are we ready to do it? Let's go. But it kept going slower and slower until it never actually got out. My mom asked the following question which I never even considered. Do they hate you?

They don't. This is what innovation does in an organization. When you try to do something new, people are unsure of how it's going to play out, and everybody wants to put their hands in it. It's exciting at the same time, it's difficult to imagine the future. So, when you try to put somebody on edge and do something in a new way, it's going to create a situation where everything is going to slow down to a snail's pace. And there are likely going to be people who are going to act against you behind the scenes, and you may never even know about them.

When you run across red tape as a shark you need to:

- Stay positive
- Stay on task
- Get it done, even if it isn't perfect, if it is done it is a win
- Get that f-ing grant proposal out on time.

C. Entropy is Always a Slog

The second law of thermodynamics has been written in many different forms. In my opinion, the simplest way states something like – the change in the entropy (the system's disorder) of a closed system will be greater or equal to zero. To translate it, unless you apply an external action (like work) your room will always get messier. People have tried to argue with this law for a long time, yet the 2nd law always wins.

Now let's put this into context with a statement I hear students say all the time. "I am going to put this down and pick it up later." What a loaded statement!

In some cases, this can be a very good thing. As I mentioned before, some of my best ideas come in the shower, or sleeping, or out for a walk. When I am stuck on a very difficult problem, sometimes it pays to take some time away and focus on something else for a while. While we move on to other things, our brain, processing in the background, is working through the problem.

However, the longer you are away from a project, the more entropy has a chance to take over.

For example, do you remember all the little details of a paper you wrote a month ago? Do you remember why a seemingly good idea is an unsuccessful one? Do you remember where you put everything in the lab or on your desk? We tend to lose these things when we step away from a problem for a long time.

Our atomic physics experiments in the lab involve very sensitive laser alignments. These experiments are so sensitive that changes in temperature, humidity, or even a nearby train can have meaningful effects on the experiment. As a researcher, I have found that the longer one goes between measurements, the more the experimental systems become out of alignment. These things take time to fix and realign. Thus, the longer I went between measurements, the more time I had to spend to get the system working again. Sometimes, going away for a week, would require an entire extra week to get the experiment set back up. This is just part of what makes discovery and innovation so hard. Sometimes you just have to deal with it. When things work, we don't leave the lab and take as much data as possible.

I find that keeping the word "entropy" in mind is important. If things are going well, I am going to find every opportunity to take advantage of the situation because we are all fighting against entropy. If you walk away from perfect conditions, you never know when you will get it all perfect again.

D. Be Persistent

A shark is both persistent and patient. The reality is that when you try to do anything, people will always throw up road blocks. You have to find a way to persist.

When I was a young professor, I was assigned to co-chair a conference on campus. It was a hoot and a crap ton of work. The English department was having a reading as part of the conference – that is where people read excerpts from the works they have made – a big deal in the creative folks' circles. I wanted to make the space as comfortable and as amazing as possible. In the room next door there were a number of sofas and comfy chairs that were not being used – in perfect condition. I thought what could be better, let's move the comfy furniture from one room to the next. That way the English folks would be able to be comfy cozy for their event.

So, I went through the proper channels and was told absolutely not. You can't move furniture from one room to the next. I was like WTF? So, I asked formally again, this time going up the food chain and asking the big cheese. Around my university I find that I usually have to ask three times before I get a Yes answer. Are they kind of daring me to ask three times? Don't they know I am going to ask as many times as I can until I learn why my request isn't reasonable?

In this case, my request was denied three times. The only answer I got was "because"! What was up with that? Because that is a terrible answer. This time it turned out there was some issue with the union and moving things. And I do support the unions. I belong to one and happily enjoy the benefits they give. But when simple easy requests are denied because of simple union issues, likely, as it was in this case, someone just didn't want to do it. In cases like this, it is difficult to be 100% supportive of workers. (I support workers getting the job done. And we need to pay people more. A lot more! And give more vacation time – except in universities, they already have enough. And then encourage people to work hard and get things done. The basics always need to get done.)

Oh, it's time for my favorite - Ask for forgiveness not permission. This is tricky because you are taking a risk. An unforeseen safety issue might pop up and bite you – this has absolutely happened to me more than once. So be careful when applying this advice.

I woke up the day of the conference, came in early, and moved the damned sofas into the room myself. Afterwards, I got yelled at. No biggie. I was nice about it. And I tried to do the work myself. Once the workers saw me moving the sofas they came over and helped. I got my way. Those who go for it usually get their way.

The key thing was that I was ultimately nice about it with the office. I kind of played it off as I was trying to make the place better. Ten years, I still have an amazing relationship with that office. Do they always say Yes to my requests? Absolutely not. But now, I get a detailed explanation for why my idea will or will not work. I don't get the "no" just because.

So, I am saying to cry and cry and cry until the spoiled brat gets his toy, sure. Especially today, the system is designed for maximum efficiency. If you want to do something different, you are going to have to be aggressive (and still nice) and make that shit happen! Be a shark, yo!

E. Not Mindless, Process - Data - Informed

Getting back to Gary Vee – man I love that guy. He tells folks to keep working hard and be persistent. He says that if you keep working at your dreams, they can come true. That's when some kid gets up and asks, "But I have been making <insert social media post type> for one year and I still only have a handful of followers on <whatever social media platform>." Gary Vee looks at them and asks if they are doing the same thing every day? Which on my TikTok feed the person says yes. That's when Gary Vee goes on a rant about how you have to keep innovating, trying new things, and do the things people like and don't do the things people don't like. So obvious. Yet so difficult. Social media is insane.

The other buzz word for those of us that have been around for a while is "Fail Fast". The idea is simple. You got to try out new ideas of course. And you want to see if they will be a success. Try to make it work! See what happens. Use data and metrics to evaluate if the thing you are trying is working. And when you have data that says such a thing is a failure: drop it and move on. Of course, no one wants to fail, but if you do, fail quickly so you use up as few resources as possible.,

Wait! This seems like an oxymoron. You are correct. In one breath I am saying you have to be patient with your ideas. In the other breath, I am saying you have to fail fast. But the trick is in the details. You need to have metrics (even if they are qualitative) that give you feedback on how you are doing. You need to be listening to what the data from these metrics are telling you. And use them to guide your decisions. But use caution here, sometimes quality data comes from sources other than the metrics you initially felt were important; make sure to be flexible and look at data from all sources. If things are working, you have to be patient with the process even if they aren't maximal yet.

Consider the following example. My wife started a butterfly mobile company. She made amazingly beautiful mobiles with a variety of crafting tools around the house. At one point, there was no place to sit in our living room, only butterfly mobiles. They were all over. I tried to sit on the chair to watch some TV. I carefully moved the two or three mobiles on the chair elsewhere somehow. I sat down in the seat and I realized I won't be able to watch the TV because there were 10 mobiles blocking my view. They took over our house.

She spent a couple of months selling them. What we found was that you could sell them for about $25 a piece. At that price, they sold like hot cakes. But if she raised the price to even $30 then no one bought them. They cost a lot to make, around $15 a piece, and that didn't even include the time she spent on them. When we figured her costs, time, and revenue, she was making something like $6 a day.

That is important data. In order to make this into a business, she would have had to make serious improvements in the process of making these mobiles to bring down the unit price. The selling price was set at $25 apiece.

Now, here is where the shark mentality helps. Make a decision and stick with it. She decided that it wasn't worth it to make those improvements. Sometimes you can figure this information by doing some calculations with research. Sometimes you have to try it for yourself. Then, dive in. Start! Make something happen! Then use your data to help you to decide what you should do next.

Afterwards, my wife has had her hand in a number of successful startup opportunities. I am so happy she didn't turn our house into a long-term butterfly mobile factory. But I am really happy she dived into this project. She learned so much and now we have a number of butterfly mobiles decorating the house. Doing something is usually more productive than not doing anything at all. At the same time, you have to be adaptive and listen to the data (and messages) the world around is giving you.

Chapter 7 Takeaways

Red tape and difficult problems will slow you down. These can derail even the most wonderful ideas.

You have to be persistent as you work through the problems and bureaucracy, continually using the data to inform your decisions. Sometimes, the data is so overwhelming, you have to just listen to it and move on.

8 HUNT IN GROUPS – BUILD YOUR TEAMWORK SKILLS – ITS WHAT EMPLOYERS ARE LOOKING FOR

I was today years old when I learned that hammerhead sharks hunt in packs. How awesome is that? How scary is that? Imagine being surrounded by a pack of hammerhead sharks swimming around you, circling you, above you, below you. Holy cow that sounds like an actual nightmare I had last week.

Can you imagine? The more hammerhead sharks, the scarier it is. While that might not be good from the point of view of the prey, it most definitely is good for the sharks. To their point of view, this all just sounds like they are going to sit down with their family for a tasty meal (i.e., you).

Working in a group can make you more powerful – as long as you work together.

A. Blood in the Water Attack

I learned somewhere that sharks can smell blood from very far away. That's scary. If you have a little bit of blood in the water, sharks are going to come and get you. It always makes me nervous when I go swimming in shark infested waters in Long Island, NY. Thinking about this in terms of careers, whenever there is opportunity, the sharks are going to be out to get the opportunity. You need to be prepared to move and seize your chance, or someone else will get there before you.

I am a control freak. I also have obsessive-compulsive disorder (OCD). So, when I do important things, I want to make sure they are 100% right. And I don't trust things unless I see it with my own eyes. This makes working in a group difficult, as you can imagine. Actually, this makes *leading* a team even harder. When you are only a team-member you only have to work on your part, but when you are leading a team, you are responsible for every part.

I think a lot of people who are in similar shoes either micromanage or do the work themselves. I tend to lean toward the latter. I tend to try to take on as much of the responsibility as I can. At least then I can be sure that I dotted all my ts and crossed all my Is. I say that joking, but sometimes when you're overworked it's easier to make mistakes. Then you aren't so perfect anymore.

Regardless of my own limitations, working in a group is better, in the long run. It is more scalable. What do I mean when I use the word "scalable" here? Even if you are amazing, there is a physical limit to how much you can do and/or directly manage in one week. However, if you create a working structure that allows for other people to do the work (and/or manage), this can apply in a company of a few people, but it could also apply to a company with thousands of people. When you are first working on a project, sometimes you feel you need to do everything. As whatever enterprise you are working on becomes bigger, at some point you are going to have to let go and let other people take some of the responsibility. Having a "scalable" approach to your business is super helpful, because it allows this to happen "more" easily – it's never easy for me to let go.

Obviously, a company like Google or Apple, requires many different employees who work at various levels on various things and are empowered to do their jobs. (The CEO is not responsible for them getting their work done.) But they all have to do their jobs for the company to be successful.

Sharks set up ourselves to be movers and shakers. It is true that we have to be able to take on everything to make things happen. But we also have to be able work with groups, inspire people to contribute, and manage competing interests. As someone who frequently works in non-profit spaces, you often have to do this without paying members of your team. We need to do this because we are going to need a following in order to make an impact bigger than just ourselves.

As sharks, we need to create a vision of what we want to do. Other people are going to be going about what they do and likely they are going to have agendas that are different than your agenda. We have to be okay with that. This is not always the easiest thing to do.

One of the ways we can get people on our side and to get the people to move as a team is to have a clear vision of what you are trying to accomplish. And then to advocate for your vision. As you get feedback from people who you would like to work with, find ways to connect their mission statement to your vision. Be clear and direct. Be open to criticism. Make it a continuous conversation.

For example, my vision of what I want to accomplish with my research lab is to, "create leaders and develop the skills of future leaders through real atomic physics experiments." While atomic physics experiments sound scary, what I really mean is "lasers" – which is totally badass! Then if I am talking with a political science student who wants to be a doctor, who I think would do well working in the lab, I say, my vision is developing critical thinkers. To be successful in medicine you will want to be a good critical thinker. What about coming to work in my lab?

That was the actual scenario in which we got an amazing student to volunteer in my lab. We even got a couple of publications off of his work. He was amazing. He knew what my vision was. This vision was aligned to what he wanted to do, and then we were able to work together. And because we both slightly aligned our separate visions of our future, we were able to come together to get a lot done and partly launch his career forward. (Listen there aren't too many political science majors applying to medical school with a peer-reviewed quantum mechanics paper. No one is going to doubt this student's ability to learn and excel at new things.)

In group projects, I often think that people don't go through this part of asking what the vision is. They just dive in. The problem is that students in the group are struggling to make group projects work. Starting off with what you want to get out of the project is a really good start.

If someone in the group says, "I just want to get a C on this project and do the least amount possible." We, as group mates, can't be upset at them when they don't stay up all night trying to make the project perfect. They have told you they don't want to do that.

How would a shark group member deal with this? They might give a rousing speech about how important this project is to their future and try to get buy in from the C-student. There are definitely times where this might work. Especially if the student has expressed interest in not being a C student before. However, it is more likely that those words will fall on deaf ears.

A better solution might be to agree on:
- A framework of responsibility you are going to do on the project to be handed in with the project
- Your team's expectations of reward versus work put into the project. The A students can be assured that they will get the maximum credit and acknowledgement of their work. Likewise, the C-students can set themselves up with a reasonable amount of work for the effort they want to do. For example, don't ask the C-student to contribute 33% to the main idea for a project in a group of three. Develop a plan and give them something they would enjoy doing, such as using ChatGPT or Google to dig up associated research.

In general, we do want to bring everyone along with us and get the maximum effort from all of the people we are working with. Even if one student only puts in a little bit of effort, they will to do some, and in most cases that is good enough.

B. Change Your Perspective

Now an A student might say, "whoa wait a minute here. You are saying that it is okay that people might do different amounts of work and the professor might give us the same high grade. That doesn't seem fair."

The difficult reality is that life isn't fair. The C student may only be willing to do C level work. And the A student demands A level work. Is it reasonable for the A level student to demand the C level student to do A level work? In fact, for a host of reasons, it might be impossible for the C level student to do the work. That might have to do with the time they have available, family concerns beyond their control, etc.

As a shark, it is your responsibility to look out for yourself and your own interest. If you feel you need the A, it might be necessary for you to make that A happen. Your goal is to maximize the contribution of your teammates, so you get the most amount of useful effort from them.

Being mean to the C level student on the team isn't going to encourage that team member to do more on their group project. Whereas being encouraging to your team members and asking them to do what they can is helpful, and more likely to keep them coming back for more. Being encouraging and positive might also motivate your team members. While it isn't likely to make them do anything they don't want to, they might come to see working with you as an opportunity to improve their situation in the class.

A successful shark gets the A, has a good team dynamic, and tries to get the most effort out of his team members.

C. The Dreaded Group Project

One of the things that I have learned in my 12 years of being a professor is that students hate group projects. Maybe hate isn't a strong enough word to describe how students feel. When I assign the group projects, you can be sure that I am going to have a couple of groups in my office yelling at me (possibly each other) about how the project is going.

So why do I assign group projects in my classes? Because I basically view college as practice for the real world. And in almost every job I have had, I have found that I am primarily evaluated on my work in a team. It is often impossible to separate out the work that I am doing with the work that my team is doing. Everyone has to do a stellar job in order for the project to be successful. I assign these projects because I want to prepare students for this inevitability.

If your group is failing, no matter how amazing you are, the amount by which you are going to get rewarded is diminished. Conversely, if your group is amazing and you are not a superstar, you are likely going to see a boost in your reward. Simply put, groups are critical to success.

Of course, some groups are terrible and some people will decide to not pull their weight. At the same time, there can be someone on the other end who is pushing too hard or too much. Often times, I will hear people say, I am happy to do all of the work, I just don't want person X – who did no work, to get any of the credit.

Once I hear that, I can tell that the group has failed, although it's not clear where that failure is coming from. It is likely coming from everyone on the team. Once people are calling each other out, it's over.

So, what do you do if you have a group member that isn't doing their work? You should tell the teacher. Rather than calling out your teammate, ask them for help. I would imagine this to be a healthy way to broach the subject:

> Professor Wright, do you have a moment?
>
> ...
>
> As you know, myself and Person Y and Z have been assigned to work on this project for your class. We started a group email chat after the project was assigned. We have sent a couple of emails requesting setting up a time to meet and have not heard from Person Z. So, during Monday's class, I asked Person Z when they could meet and they said Friday in the library at 2pm. So as soon as we agreed, I sent them a calendar invite. Z didn't come and again its radio silence. Y and I met and started planning the project, but without Z's input. Can you please help us get back on track?

Notice that the student tried to reach out a number of different times and a number of different ways. When they caught them in person and got them to commit to a date, they immediately set up the appointment. All the while documenting things in email and calendar. They are not whining about how terrible Z is or about how their lives/grades are going to be affected.

However, they did what is needed for their project to succeed (and grades to be high) and straightforward asked their instructor for help.

Their professor might not do anything, but I think this is an amazing start.

D. Work in Symbiotic Relationships, Pilot Fish

Pilot fish are great. They swim around the sharks eating left over waste while keeping the sharks clean. This symbiotic relationship is good for both the sharks and the pilot fish. The pilot fish gets a rich diet from the shark and protection. The shark stays clean and healthy. We need to build relationships like this with the people we work with.

I remember when I was mentoring a student who was doing a research project. I helped her to put together the project, secure funding, and gave her some ideas with how she arranged the data. I was helping her put together an abstract for a presentation she was going to give at a conference. I said, "put my name next to yours on the author list." The student looked at me and said, "NO! You didn't do any of the work on the project."

I laughed! It was a funny conversation. She was both right and very wrong. It is true that I, as the professor, did not take any of the actual data on the project, or write the presentation, or even do any of the experiments. That said, I did make the environment for this student to be successful. It took time and effort.

It is important to reward people you work with and to work symbiotically with them. There are things that a junior team member researcher has to do for a project to work. There are also things that a professor has to do to make a project work. When it comes time to publish, the student who did the lion's share of the work should get a lion's share of the credit and whatever rewards are given for what thing is being worked on. As a professor, I make sure this happens as much as possible: giving the students who do all of the work on the project all of the credit.

But a small amount of the credit does have to be shared by the research team and professors. While there are situations where there might actually be a single author for a paper, I usually think it is a good idea to share the prestige of the article as much as possible.

Another situation might be a junior and a senior student working on the project. While not always, usually the senior student understands the project deeper and understands how to overcome its failures. This student tends to have done more on the project. When it comes time to list who worked on the research project, the senior student is likely going to have the place of honor among the listed authors on the publication. In my field of atomic physics, this is the first author. The other authors are listed, of course, but they are second to the student who has done the most. Science is about working together and building consensus, says Naomi Oreskes in her book Why Trust Science. To be successful in STEM and as a shark, you have to work together to be successful, and sometimes that means taking a long a pilot fish or even being someone's pilot fish while you learn the ropes.

E. Make a Project Plan

When I teach classes that require a group project, I always provide a template for a project plan. I have my students make one for their project. The students have to have a meeting with me and all agree with the project plan before they can start it.

In making a project plan, the teammates on the project write out as many tasks as possible that are required for the project. This is good for many different reasons. It helps to draw out all of the necessary steps to get a project done. Sometimes, we forget how long certain tasks take and how difficult they can be. Taking a moment at the beginning of the project to think about these is key to having the best experience and project deliverable as possible, with the least amount of work.

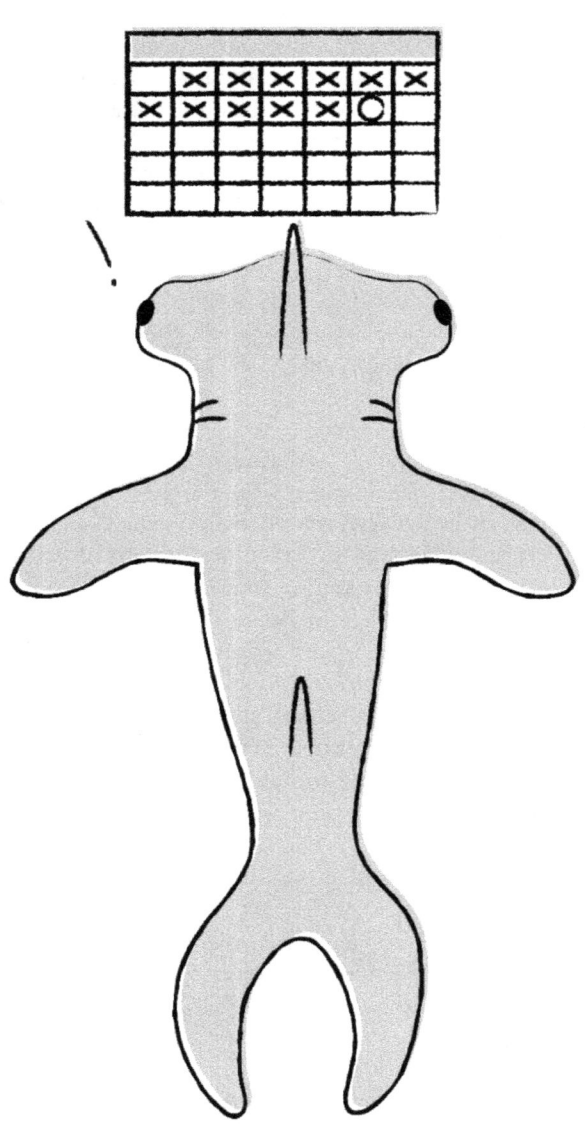

Table 1 - Example of a part of a Project Plan outlining different phases for the plan, dividing up the roles into tasks, who is responsible, and the all-important deadline

Phase	Task	Who	Due
Initial Research	Kick Off Meeting	All	April 1st
	Meeting Notes	Kelly	April 2nd
	Updates to Meeting Notes	Zoya and Katie	April 3rd
	Textbook Summary of Teaching Assignment	Zoya	April 3rd
Project Plan	Draft Project Plan	Katie	April 4th
	Review of Plan – 1	Kelly	April 4th
	Review of Plan – 2	Zoya	April 4th
	Finalize Project Plan	Katie	April 4th
	Make Project Map	Katie	April 4th
Research	Develop a source list	Zoya	April 5th
...	...	...	...

Typically project plans are done in a spreadsheet program (like Excel); however, I think this is the perfect use case for Google Sheets. The shareability of Google Sheets will allow everyone on the project a chance to use and make changes to the project plan; thus, making it a dynamic tool. At a minimum, a project plan should have at least four different columns: project phase, task, who, due. In general, it is good to have a specific person responsible for each task and a specific time.

In general, it is important to assign the task to a specific person or group of people. Sit down with your team and agree on what tasks you are going to work on. Be honest with the team, and make sure your plan is reasonable to do in the time you have. Again, don't assign the C student to a critical piece of the project before anyone else can do any of the work. That is a recipe for disaster. There is always a caveat. If a C-level student is genuinely trying to make a change and raise their game, then I think we have to watch out for this and make the student do this. This is tricky. As a college professor, I am always checking in with people and asking them what they want to get out of a project. If needed, I might help the group restructure their project plan. If the project plan doesn't make sense or isn't reasonable after you make it, don't be surprised. This often happens. This is a sign that your project plan/scope needs to be redefined. This might be a time to reach out to your professor. Bring your spreadsheet; she will be impressed with the level of thought you have put into your project.

Also don't worry about whether your project plan is perfect or not. Trust me, it's not. Project plans are a first draft of how the project will go. Almost no projects go on time and/or nicely by your step-by-step process. There will be things you missed or things that you overestimated when you were building the project. That's ok. It's not supposed to be perfect. It's a tool to get started on the project and take it to a successful end.

I can hear a student scoffing, "I don't do stupid project plans". Trust me, you do. Or rather, you will. This is how businesses managers plan their work time in a successful way. As a professional, working on projects, you are going to be assigned to work on projects, and as you move up in your career you will even be responsible for preparing project plans for your team. There is a host of amazing software that make this process easier, scalable, and provide useful analytics. I have always been partial to the work that Atlassian does. Atlassian makes a number of software tools for project management and software developers. I have always been happy with their tool JIRA. But as someone who is just getting started and working on simple, relatively straightforward projects, I think you can benefit from doing everything by hand on Google Sheets. JIRA and other software tools have so many bells and whistles that it can be overwhelming to someone who is just starting.

Do you make the project plan for your team? You are the shark, right? That is complicated. In general, I find that the most successful projects are ones that are built with everyone's input. I would rather that this project plan was built by the entire team with input from everyone. When one person starts telling people what to do, I have found it makes the people in the group – especially those C students – less likely to engage with the project in a meaningful way. You will start to hear words like "Bossy". There are times when one student might be in a leadership role, such as being the senior student in a research lab, that it might make sense for them to prepare a draft of the project plan before discussing, and importantly, editing it with the entire team.

Make sure this is done very early in the project. Find a time everyone is there. If your professor gives you time in class to work on it, I would be a very aggressive with using the class time to complete the project plan. It is often very hard for people to get together outside of class.

In addition to a project plan, I also recommend the students make a project map. The project map is a summary of the project plan that turns it into an image. Each bar refers to a high-level summary task that is plotted as a function of time. It is both an indication of how long a project will take and also an indication of when it should be started/ended. An example is shown below.

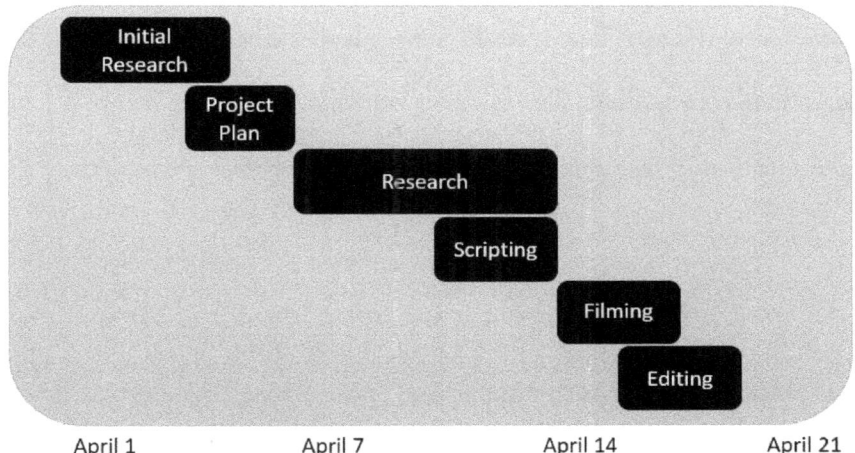

Figure 1 - An example of a Project Map.

Note that this is pretty high level. What I like about it, is that it gives you a quick update on how you are doing on a project.

Project management is a hugely developed field with tips and tricks and rules and philosophies. It is so helpful to be able to put order to a complicated, messy problem. Learning about this was one of the best parts of being a management consultant. I personally find the idea of RACI charts to be amazing. In addition to assigning who will work on a task, implementing RACI allows a project manager to assign who is (R)esponsible, (A)ccountable, (C)onsulted, and (I)nformed for each task on your project plan. Using the RACI helps to make sure you get the people side of a problem correct. It is beyond the scope of this book, but I love it so much I thought I would bring it up.

Chapter 8 Takeaways:

Sharks can get a lot done, but to scale you need to be able to work on teams

Practice, practice, practice teamwork

Find ways to motivate your mates to achieve higher goals.

Incorporate your team's ability/desire to work and make adjustments.

Make a plan and dynamically alter the plan to keep up with the project.

9 ORDERS OF THINKING

So how do you be thorough? What does that actually mean? It is both easier and more complicated than you might think. Let's break it down.

When you start investigating a problem or something you want to do, it usually pays to break things down into various "orders" of thinking. For this discussion let's talk about three separate orders, although this line of thinking can be applied to literally infinite orders of thought.

0th Order Thinking:
I spend a lot of time in my introductory classes teaching what's called back-of-the-envelope calculations. The idea here is to make an educated guess at a solution to a problem that you are working on by doing simple calculations. In fact, the calculations can be so simple you could do them on the back of an envelope.

When you're watching the recent blockbuster movie on Robert Oppenheimer, watch Enrico Fermi during the first test of the nuclear bomb. He was in the background. But he was doing something pretty amazing and if you look carefully, you can catch it. He was dropping paper (or "dust") to see how far the blast wave pushed paper on its way to the ground. From this, he was able to quickly estimate the power of the explosion. Analyzing all of the data with the entire Manhattan project team, they were able to get a fairly precise answer. But that all took time, lots of resources, and was expensive. Many times, it can take years to do a study like this. The thing is that by watching dust fall to the ground, Enrico Fermi was able to get an educated guess on how big that explosion actually was in moments after the blast. Thus, sometimes back-of-the-envelope calculations are called Fermi problems.

These quick approaches to problems are very useful both in and out of physics, because they help people quickly check to see if ideas are worth exploring in greater detail. I will often use them to sanity check a measurement we made in the lab. If our numbers don't match what we expect, I start asking myself and the team more detailed questions about our experiment and set up.

In business, this skill is necessary. There, people are bombarded with investment opportunities. Choosing which one you should invest in seems almost impossible. Even knowing which investments you should spend time researching can be difficult. Back-of-the-envelope calculations are great because you can make quick, sort-of scientifically backed decisions without losing too much time.

The example I often ask the students to do in class is to imagine that someone says they are going to open a pizza place on campus and they need $5,000 of your money as an investment. And they claim that if they can sell 8,000 pizzas in one year they will break even. Add any more pizzas and they will be able to start paying you back with interest.

Should you invest? Good question. Is it reasonable that they could sell 5,000 pizzas? Let's see.

The goal to solving back-of-the-envelope calculations is to break things down into small manageable numbers that you can make a reasonable guess at, and then use the units of those numbers to sort out how something should be calculated. The whole thing is a guess! But it is surprisingly useful. Here's my answer:

Be A Shark

Here is some information that I might already know about the school I was at:

- 1,000 students
- 30 weeks / year - College is only on campus for a portion of the year
- 2 slices / week per student – Okay this was a complete guess. But a reasonable one. I had pizza last Friday for dinner and had three slices. I don't eat pizza often, only about once every two weeks. But some people will eat more than me. Some might not eat pizza at all. This is just a guess. Don't get too worried about the exact number. Just get a "reasonable" number.
- 1 pie has about 10 slices

So:

$$\frac{2 \; slice}{week \; student} \; \frac{1 \; pie}{10 \; slices} \; \frac{30 \; weeks}{year} \times 1000 \; students \rightarrow 6,000 \; \frac{pies}{year}$$

Don't invest! They need to corner the entire market of students eating pizza for them to even break even. And that isn't likely to happen, at least not at first.

Notice a couple of things that I did here. I didn't spend time getting the numbers exactly right. I made a quick guess on slices per week per student. But that was only a guess and I didn't spend more than a few seconds on it - literally the time it took me to type the sentence on my computer. Could it have been 3 or 4 slices per person? For sure. But it isn't 100 slices per person or even 20. It might be reasonable for someone to order 20 slices or even a 100 per week but they are going to be an exception. Two gives you the order of magnitude guess.

The same goes for the number of slices a pizza pie has. I believe the number is typically 8, but 8 is a difficult number to calculate. Like seriously who actually knows what 8 X 7 is? Ok, you need to know what 8 X 7 is. But can you tell me what is 8 X 7 X 13 X 6 X 1/4? Ok, I used a calculator, its 1092. Multiplying by powers of 10s is much easier. 10 X 10 X 10 X 6/4 ~ 1000. 1000 is the same as 1092 when you are guessing. Just consider all the variation in the different kinds of pizzas and different kinds of slices. Since we are estimating it really doesn't matter too much.

Your answer isn't going to be too precise. In fact, it just tells us the order of magnitude of the number we are looking at. The number could be 3000 pizzas or 7000 pizzas but it isn't 20,000 pizzas, 700,000 pizzas, or 10 pizzas. Knowing this order of magnitude for your result is important because it gives us an educated guess on the answer.

During the first week of school, I find that students write their answers to exactly whatever the calculator says. For example, they might do a calculation and write down 6780.2481073 pizzas. I always ask them how sure they are about that last 3. To which, the new students says, I got it perfectly right, see my calculator. But the thing is, that the numbers that went into this calculation are already imprecise (they are guesses) or quick measurements like Fermi's experiment, there is no way you would even believe the first 7 and maybe not even the first 6. It's a guess!

The classic problem that management consultants consider during interviews is "How many piano tuners are there in Chicago". Take a moment to google the problem. It has been solved a number of different ways. The gist is that you start with what you know and then start to build your way toward an educated guess.

A lot of students say, but what if I don't know anything. This happens often when I ask them how many drops of water are in Long Island Sound. The first question is, what is Long Island Sound? You know that small body of water between Connecticut and Long Island, NY which is the same size as a great lake. So, once we get going, they will say, that's pretty big, maybe 500 drops. At this point I am literally pulling my hair out of my head. They are looking at me as if I am from another planet.

The world is made up of numbers. Take a look around and see what's going on around. Ask yourself questions, for example how many people are on this train I am taking. Or how many cars are there on this highway? Make it a game. The more of these questions you do, the better you get. But also, the more likely you are going to be aware of things that are happening around you – which you can use to solve more difficult problems.

This 0th order thinking helps you to understand the scale of the problem you are working on. For example,

- How precise do you have to be to make a measurement?
- How much money are you going to need?
- How long do you have to wait?

The gist is that you start with what you know and then start to build your way toward an educated guess.

1st Order Thinking:
First order thinking is what we typically do in our science classes in school.

Be A Shark

The first step is to identify the main fundamental principle that is driving a problem. Then use that principal to make a prediction of what's going to happen, and do experiments to test out that prediction. The big consideration here is that you ignore some of the other details that you might need to consider to get a perfect solution to the problem you are trying to work on. You only apply the big fundamental ideas. A really good example is looking at the trajectory of a falling object. This is a standard Physics I teaching lab. You can determine all of the usual numbers in the lab by using only the gravitational force and neglecting air resistance. Air resistance is still there. It's just small enough that if you don't worry about it, it will not affect your numbers too much.

This is often very successful because of what I call the 80/20 rule. You get 80% of the results with 20% of the effort. To get every single detail right and master every single effect, it is going to take a lot of work. Don't do it (just yet). Just get the big things right and try to solve using these fundamental ideas. Most of the time this will work just fine.

This is exactly how the most recent versions of AI work. They assume that variables vary linearly - which they most always do if you look close enough. It applies that principle to a large data set and makes a prediction as to what the answer should be. The answer isn't always going to be right, but it will likely be close.

Higher-Order Thinking:
This is a loaded phrase and can mean many different things. Here I use the term to refer to getting all the details right: hunting down every little thing that doesn't match and figuring out why.

You have to be relentless. It is not enough to say that my theory sort of matches my data. You have to hunt each discrepancy and find out what each wiggle is.

My favorite paper that I ever worked on was "Collective Oscillations of the Radial Quadrupole Mode in the BEC-BCS Crossover." We used laser cooled Lithium atoms to look at strongly interacting fermions and asked do these atoms act collectively? They did and it was more interesting than we first thought. Initially we thought, hey this is kind of boring, the gas can oscillate two different ways and it does depend on the details of the experiment. But what initially threw us for a loop was how much detail and exciting information we were able to extract from the data.

Here's the data we published:

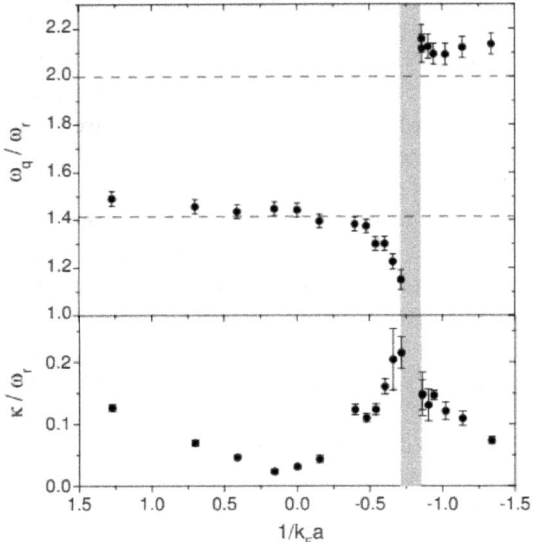

FIG. 5. Frequency ω_q (upper plot) and damping rate κ (lower plot) of the radial quadrupole mode. Both quantities are normalized to the radial trap frequency ω_r and plotted versus the interaction parameter $1/k_Fa$. The dashed lines indicate the theoretical predictions in the hydrodynamic ($\omega_q/\omega_r = \sqrt{2}$) and in the collisionless limit ($\omega_q/\omega_r = 2$). The shaded area marks the transition from hydrodynamic to collisionless behavior between $1/k_Fa \approx -0.72$ ($B \approx 930$ G) and $1/k_Fa \approx -0.85$ ($B \approx 960$ G).

Figure 2 - Figure and caption taken from A. Altmeyer, S. Riedl, C. Kohstall, M.J. Wright, J. Hecker Denschlag, and R. Grimm, Collective Oscillations of the Radial Quadrupole Mode in the BEC-BCS Crossover. Phys. Rev. A 76, 033610 (2007).

The details of this plot are unimportant to the discussion. There were two frequencies. $\omega = 1.4\omega_r$ and $\omega = 2.0\omega_r$ indicated by the dashed lines in the top figure. One can see from the graph above that the data dots sort of match the prediction (dashed lines). And we could have been done there. They Agree! Woo-Hoo! Our experiments and theory agree. We understand. These experiments are difficult to do. Ours roughly agreed with experiment, we could have wiped our hands of this and gone on to the next thing. That is not what we did. We dove in.

We tried to find out every detail about what was going on. We looked at the graph and asked questions like why are there small deviations. We kept digging out information and by the end we had not only understood this piece of information but many, many more. So, I have published papers that have a higher impact factor (a rating for journal articles) than this one, but I am so very proud of this paper. We just kept digging into the data and in the end, we could tell a much bigger, much better story of how the universe works.

Of course. we had an amazing team. Dr. Grimm and Dr. Hecker Denschlag are two amazing professors in Europe that have long, amazing careers with huge lists of publications. Dr. Altmeyer is an executive at Deutsche Bahn (very important German railroad company), Dr. Riedl is an engineer at Airbus, and Dr. Kohstall is the founder and builder of Kind Humanoid. (Google Dr. Kohstall and be prepared to be amazed).

When you approach a problem in science, finance, or in your daily life it is a good idea to use elements of 0th order thinking, 1st order thinking, and higher order thinking. There is no algorithm for determining how or when you use these methods. You have need to employ all three of these methods of thinking simultaneously. Always asking yourself if every thing is self consistent. If it is, it is a way to know that your answer is likely right or that you are moving in the right direction. If it isn't, you have to dive in more deeply until you understand why it is behaving that way.

In physics we have a mechanism for how we think about these various "orders" of thinking. Listen if math terrifies you, please skip the next few paragraphs. That said I am a physics professor here we go. The idea is called Taylor series. We are able to construct a mathematical function f(x) by breaking it down in pieces.

The mathematical expression is given as something like:

$$f(x) = f(0) + \frac{x}{1!} f'(0) + \frac{x^2}{2!} f''(0) + \frac{x^3}{3!} f'''(0) + \dots$$

0th Order Thinking:
We can get a quick estimate of what $f(x)$ if we know what the value is at one point (any point), but let's call it $x = 0$ here. It is likely not going to be correct but it is likely close to the value, especially if the value of x is near 0.

1st Order Thinking:
In this case we can ask ourselves the following question, how does $f(x)$ change with x? In algebra and statistics, we call this the slope and in calculus we call this the derivative.

$$f'(0) \sim \frac{\Delta f}{\Delta x}$$

When we write down the following equation.

Be A Shark

$$f(x) \sim f(0) + \frac{x}{1!} f'(0)$$

We are making a reasonable estimation what $f(x)$ is by using the 0th order term and then slope times the distance x.

It's likely not correct, but: it is fast and more correct than the 0th order thinking and a reasonable guess if x is small.

Higher-Order Thinking:
Using approximations in mathematics is tricky and involves years of practice to hone your skills. How many of these terms do you actually to be able to express $f(x)$. This depends on the specific situation.

In general, the answer is all of them. The expansion goes on forever and you need to include every single term in order to understand every single detail. But by breaking it down into small meaningful pieces, we can learn a lot about a situation we are trying to solve.

Be A Shark

10 BE RELENTLESS

A. Make Situations Fun

Do you ever notice how when you play a good video game, you can play it for hours without even noticing? Major video game bosses can cause stressful situations, causing you to yell out four-letter words, and countless hours of frustration. And you keep doing it for hour after hour, overcoming one major difficulty after another until you get to the finish line. Sometimes problems are so difficult that you are unable to find solutions by yourself, so you look up solutions on the internet and YouTube. Then that same student walks into the lab and tries one simple thing with a laser, and cries it's too hard and demands that I do the experiment for them, without even breaking a sweat.

AAAARRRRRRGGGGGGGHHHHHHH.

This is a hot button issue for me as a professor. To be clear, I don't mind helping students solve problems. It is why I became a professor. But it is important for the students to try to overcome their issues themselves before I give them help – just like you do every night when you play video games.

Since when do you ask your parent how to solve a particular level of a video game?

This is a point in your educational journey when you can use your creativity and turn your tasks into games. Make your work fun. There is no reason you can't. Here are some ideas.

Be A Shark

- Have small, friendly competitions with your peeps or co-workers.
- Set a goal for the day - like I am going to get 80% of the light through that optical fiber today – and give yourself a reward like a candy bar if you make it happen.
- Arrange your work into a video game format, with bosses you need to beat and time to prepare for beating that boss.
- Listen to fun, zany music while you work.

Turning work into a friendly competition between friends or into a competition between you and a boss can make the time fly by and make it enjoyable for you.

Be A Shark

This will make you more productive and successful.

B. Start Early

Don't procrastinate. "But I work so well under pressure." That may be the case, but you are still taking a gamble every time you procrastinate. You might not get a project done in time, or something surprising might come up beyond your control to prevent you from being successful. It is always surprising when students come to me when a project is due and ask if they can have access to the lab late at night because they haven't started their project and they have to get it done. But it's 10 pm and the project is due at midnight, and it's at least 5 hours of work.

As soon as you start a project, write down all of the tasks that you are going to need to do to get the task done. Then think about how long those tasks are going to take. Finally, schedule when you are going to do those things. And then do them at the associated times. It might only take 5 to 10 minutes. But thinking through whether you need to do something before the due date is critical! You can make sure you have the time to schedule something that is going to take a couple of hours to complete.

And when you start doing this, you will suck at it. Everyone sucks at everything when they first start. But as you do more, you will get better and better. This will make you more effective.

Of course, a student might say that they just don't care to do these things. That is fine, but that is not what a shark would say.

C. When you uncover something that seems bad, it's a good thing. It's not a bug, it's a feature

When you are working on hard things, it will not go as expected. Life has a way of always throwing you a curveball. That is okay. It's not a bug, it's a feature.

One of the more difficult things to do when solving meaty problems is deal with unexpected things. The first time something unexpected happens, it might make sense to ignore it. But if that unexpected thing keeps coming up, don't run away from it. Run towards it. It might mean more work, but in the end, it might open you up to something amazing!

Consider this story: A couple of engineers were building a large, fancy antenna in New Jersey. They had a pesky signal in their data. They couldn't figure out where it was coming from. They tried literally everything they could to figure out where this signal was coming from. They even cleaned bird crap out of their antenna because they thought it might be the issue. They were digging to try to figure out what it was.

What they were measuring was the background radiation in the universe. The temperature of that radiation was consistently 2.7K (-270 C). This measurement was the first confirmation that there was this background radiation. Where might this radiation come from? The Big Bang at the start of the universe. Bam! Can anyone say Nobel Prize? You never know when something you are doing can lead to something amazing. Keep digging.

Computer programmers would often use the line "It's not a bug it's a feature" when someone would find something odd about the computer code they had written. The idea there is that when the code was first developed it was only able to do a couple of things. Now it can do something else and you might be able to take advantage of it to do something really amazing.

Of course, most of the time, it's just a bug and you need to fix it. However, when these things happen you have to keep hunting down problems until you find out exactly how to fix the problem. You have to be relentless. Because if there is not perfect agreement then something is amiss and you need to dig it out. Once you understand all of it, there will be new ways to take advantage of this new knowledge.

PART THREE:
LAUNCHING YOUR CAREER

11 WHAT TO STUDY?

This chapter is going to be an ad for why I think Physics is the perfect major for a young shark who is trying to figure out their path in the world. Physics is a difficult major for sure. It requires a lot of math. But for students who can embody the shark mentality after they complete their degree, physics will get them to where they want to go.

Honestly, there are so many good majors out there. It doesn't matter so much which major you choose; it's about how much you care and what you do with your career. It's about how you take up opportunities that come your way. Sharks make great things happen wherever they are.

As a disclaimer, I am a physics professor.

A. Philosophy is a Great Degree

But first, let's start with philosophy and discuss why it is a great degree to get for a shark. Philosophy doesn't usually give you a computer skill like computer programming, Microsoft Excel, or how to operate a piece of machinery. But you can get lots of amazing other skills. There is one really important skill that you get – philosophy teaches you how to think.

You learn how to take someone's argument and pull it apart. You train yourself to find the missing pieces or weak parts of an idea. And it teaches you how to craft your own argument so that your peers won't be able to easily pick apart your argument. Talk about a great career skill for someone who wants to enter into the legal profession or pitch start up ideas. A degree in philosophy allows one to develop a well-crafted argument to almost any situation.

Majoring in business at the most elite schools can be a great way to start your way to the top. However, for all but a few people, it is difficult to make it to the top in corporate America unless you catch a break. There are too many glass ceilings to break through. So, to get through you need a really strong hammer: your mind. I imagine that as a business major, you spend whole courses learning how to make Pivot tables in Excel and other valuable skills. In the long run, I wonder if this is a waste of time. While small technical skills are important to succeed in a job, they are easy to learn with a couple of YouTube videos and a book or two and change frequently. Learning how to think critically and how to learn new skills is far more important.

A philosophy professor once told me that philosophy graduates don't earn high salaries right away, but later in their careers do quite well. The idea here, as I understand it, is that it takes a philosophy grad a little while to catch up on the simple skills like using Excel or whatever the business needs. But the philosophy grad is also brilliantly able to keep learning and adapting to new technologies and ways of doing business, whereas other majors who didn't spend enough time on critical thinking aren't able to keep up.

So, the philosophy grad starts to pull away. What is the secret sauce? Learning how to think critically and having a growth mindset.

As they make it higher up in the company, the problems they face are less technical and more problems that require deep thinking and critical skills to solve. So, as they become executives their critical thinking training starts to take them to even greater heights.

Not only all of that, but philosophers are just fun to talk to. They know how to ask difficult, meaty questions.

B. Physics

So, physics does much of that too, but it also does so with mathematics and experimentation. This degree not only teaches you how to think, but also gives you useful skills to launch your career into the stratosphere – literally, if you wish.

What do physicists do? Physicists try to understand how the universe works in the deepest, most fundamental way. They do this through mathematical models of very simple interactions. They start with equations like $F = ma$ and $E = mc^2$ and use these laws to predict what will happen and how to build cool new technologies.

Be A Shark

What do we study? Everything! From stars, to atoms, to molecules, to fish, to black holes, birds, subatomic particles, beads, fluids, rockets, lasers, and the universe itself. And in physics there is a mythos that no problem is too big and physicists should be able to tackle any problem on any scale. That's why physicists are usually capable of teaching any of the core physics subjects. Physicists tend to be broad thinkers who can approach problems from multiple angles (again literally). In fact, exciting new fields in technology often start as physics projects. Once they get to a certain point and there are enough people working on it, it branches out into its own field. We are starting to see this happen with quantum information at this moment.

Physicists work hard to develop the ability to look at complex problems, break those problems down to the simplest and most fundamental ideas, and then build these ideas on top of one another to be able to predict what will happen in some complex experiment. And then build the complex experiment from scratch. It is the perfect ocean for a mathematically trained shark. Many physicists take up careers in engineering, but it just doesn't stop there. Anywhere there is some interesting, difficult, meaty problem near the state of the art, there are usually physicists working on it.

It's no wonder that elite management consultant firms and Wall Street companies frequently try to cherry pick highly-trained physicists. As a group, they are brilliant problem solvers. And if you can figure out how to use lasers to monitor what happened in a black hole collision millions of years ago, then the simple problems that the local transportation company has isn't even going to make you sweat too much.

C. Must major in Physics?

Do you absolutely have to choose to major in physics if you want to be a shark? Yes! Absolutely! Again, remember I'm a physics professor. Hehe!

That is untrue. You can major in anything you like. In fact, what you major in isn't all that important to your sharky status. How you go about studying and working that is important. Like, really important.

D. Getting the High Grade in Life

I work with a lot of students who are only into managing their grade point average by doing the least amount of learning as possible. They might pursue a particular course of study because it is easy and they may get the best grades possible by making sure to take the easy class and easy professor. Getting straight As isn't a good thing unless you really earn it by overcoming major learning obstacles. I can hear someone asking, "Wait, don't you always 'earn' straight As?"

As with most things in life, the answer is both yes and no. Getting high marks is good. Most of the graduate programs, medical schools, and law schools require high grades. Employers too will likely hire you if you have higher grades. So, you definitely want to get good grades.

But you want to make sure you are really pushing yourself to earn those high grades. If you are not pushing yourself, you should take on more. Getting good grades with little effort isn't going to help you in the future. I find it weird when people choose biology over chemistry or physics as majors in school when they want to pursue a career in medicine. You will show them the data, that it is easier to get into medical school from chemistry than biology, and still the student will select biology. While I don't know for sure, I imagine based on my years of experience working with these students that some students do this because they feel that it is easier to be a biology major than mathematics and statistics – the best major for someone who wants to go into medicine according to "The Best Premed Majors to Get Into Medical School (2025)" – Shemmassian Consulting. Obviously, there are a lot of people who just like biology and that is a good thing. It is an amazing science.

Choosing Difficult Things to Challenge Yourself

This is not to imply that a biology major is easy. Being a biology major can be very difficult. As there are more students in biology programs, there is often more choice with how you approach your degree. A shark would make choices to put themselves against the best so they can improve and meet the challenge. Take the hard choices. Take the difficult professor who everyone says is an amazing teacher but gives the hard tests. Put yourself in situations where you have to rise to meet challenges. Tackle big, messy biological problems that matter to all of us.

And frankly, you can do this as a business or communications major too. There are amazing professors and support staff in the university. If you are in these majors, work with them to take on difficult challenges. If you are a business major, literally start your own business or get an internship at a company and work to make a difference. If you are a communications major, use Tiktok to create a news program on issues that you want to discuss. The point is, find out what resources you have available to you, then use them. Be fearless and take on difficult challenges.

Are you sitting around a diner, conference table, or research lab at 3 in the morning talking about exciting problems in the world with your friends, thinking about how you can make the world a better place or take advantage of an opportunity? Are you out of breath just trying to get your ideas out? Drained from working hard yet somehow empowered? Stressed yet on your tippy toes ready to be launched? If yes, then keep being a shark. If no, you got to get yourself into these situations.

There is no better feeling after playing a sport, where you gave everything you have. Win or lose, your opponent drew out your best and pushed you to your limit. I remember losing a baseball game to our cross-town rivals on the last play of the game. I had hit the ball far and was running around the bases with every ounce of strength I had. A player for the other team made an incredible catch and the game was over. It took me a moment to realize it, and when I did, I was sad of course. At the same time, I was exhilarated. I'd given everything I had. In another example, I beat a friend at a friendly 5 set tennis match over an entire afternoon. We gave every ounce of strength we had. When we were done, we just laid down on the court, trying to catch our breath.

A shark does this with their professional career too. They start businesses. They become the best doctor. They push the envelope. They search for the meaty problems. They push themselves to the limit to tackle problems.

I can see my wife out of the corner of my eye while I write this, thinking it is terrible. It seems if I am saying we need to push ourselves to exhaustion to be successful and be a shark. In one sense, this is correct. But I think you can have your cake and eat it too. It is important to push yourself. It is also important to make sure you have time to take care of yourself. You have to take lengthy breaks to regroup. And feel good about taking breaks, because you have earned them. The goal is not to work more, it is to optimize the work you get done with time spent. When you are working really hard, at some point your productivity goes down and you have to find ways to recharge to become efficient with your time.

I remember after losing 40 or so pounds and running a marathon, I took a whole week off of exercising. And while watching the football game on a Sunday afternoon, I had a gigantic pile of ribs from my favorite BBQ shop. I enjoyed every bite. I enjoyed naps. I had given what I could and pushed myself. Now it was time to recharge and be happy about it. The thing is I do this (or something similar) on Sundays even if I didn't run marathon the day before.

The fact is that when you go for the best, you have to put in the best amount of effort. If you don't practice basketball all of the time, you are not going to the NBA no matter how much talent you have. And if you don't do all of the little things to be a doctor, you are not going to medical school. To get to the top, you have to push yourself.

ChatGPT

Students immediately go to ChatGPT and AI to solve the hard problems. They do whatever ChatGPT tells them to do, and then they hand it in.

I'm actually a big fan of AI. I think that we should be taking advantage of new technologies to be successful. In fact, I am dictating the first draft of this book while driving my car. We really need to learn how to use these tools, and I encourage students – through assignments – to play with ChatGPT and other tools. We have to keep pushing through minutia to do great things. There are going to be times in your life when 'good enough' is enough. I find this to be true when filling out forms and other types of bureaucracy.

But we can't stop ourselves when we achieve 'good enough' because let's face it, in a world where AI is cheap, it costs an employer less to use it than hire you. The good enough feature of free ChatGPT that's available for everyone to use without a penny is super good. It's not perfect, but it's good. And then if you go and spend a couple hundred dollars more to get the really good AI, then you're going to be blown away. So why is somebody going to hire you? ChatGPT will do the job for free and the new advanced AI will do it for a low monthly service fee.

So as a young professional - hey that's you - you don't necessarily have to be better than AI, but you have to be competitive with AI and you have to succeed at the things that AI really isn't so good at while being thorough, creative, and able to relentlessly work through a project step-by-step to get to a meaningful output. You have to keep swimming – just like a shark (or Dory hehe).

I can already see the students in my class rolling their eyes and saying that's fine. I'll do that when I get a job. That always makes me laugh. Yes many people feel this way and step up to work hard when they get their first job. But there's a certain amount of training that you need to do at that job. You need to have already practiced and worked out the bugs. Because it's not going to be easy if you're not already somebody who can get through the minutia. You have to be ready to keep swimming no matter the challenge and the way to do that is practice, so whether you're in college, whether you're in a rock band, whether you're cleaning your room, you have to be willing to work your butt off all of the time and keep consistently going towards making the place better.

12 FINDING JOBS

When I initially started speaking about what it means to be a shark, I started by speaking about the job search. This is where I think the shark ethos is most important – though I started applying it to everything once it was developed.

In this chapter, we will discuss how the shark mentality can lead you on a successful job search. The key important factors are networking, being aggressive, and being thorough.

A. Don't be the Bad Employee

The first and foremost thing to remember when you are on the job search is that companies are looking to hire good people, but are really nervous about hiring bad people.

In fact, hiring a bad person can be the worst thing a company can do. Bad employees can really bring a company down. If they did nothing at work, that would likely be better than what a bad person will do at a company. A bad employee makes negative work, either by doing work that needs to be redone by other employees, or by causing trouble that distracts other workers from getting their jobs done.

There are bad employees of all types. What a hiring manager wants to do is to find someone who *fits* into their current work place – not always the best candidate. Does this lead to discrimination? Of course. It is definitely non-ideal, let's work together to fix it. But in the meantime, most hiring managers in a capitalist society only are incentivized to have profitable teams.

Let me be clear, this doesn't mean you can't be a pain in the ass. The best person on my team right now is a royal pain in my ass (you know who you are). Being a pain in the ass can lead to new innovations or managing things that have been forgotten. I look for "pain in the asses" when I hire. To be clear, being a pain in the ass doesn't equate to being a bad employee. I love it when people challenge me and get me to change my thinking.

Hiring managers don't want someone who is going to cause unnecessary drama – such as immediately escalating small, unimportant things to the boss. For example, a former student of mine was told not to spend a lot of money on his students when he was teaching over the summer by his boss on his first day. There were a lot of reasons for this and it is a reasonable request. The student disagreed and that is also fine. Sharing that disagreement is good too. But going immediately to the highest boss at the school to complain about how his rights were infringed upon is an overreach.

This can just weigh everything down, especially in 2025. We need to take every issue seriously and a complaint at this level causes a series of triggers where a host of people have to carefully review the case. This employee hasn't even done any work yet, and he has already gotten the entire school's administration working overtime. If the person felt they were discriminated against or they felt harassed, all of this would have been worthwhile. It is important to take complaints like this seriously. But the employee didn't feel any of that, he just wanted it his way, wanted to buy a ton of toys for his students, and wasn't listening to anyone else. This takes away from real issues that come up and need time to adjust.

So, when people are applying and interviewing for jobs, they believe that they need to demonstrate that they are the best possible person for a job. Obviously, you have to demonstrate that you are an excellent person and worthy of hiring. But I think you also have to help them manage their risk. Demonstrate that you are not going to be a bad employee.

Networking is a great way to do this. The more people you know who work at an institution, the more you can alleviate the hiring manager's fears and confirm that you are reliable, dependable, and not going to be a bad employee. As discussed before, networking is a slow process and can take years to do properly. But what often happens is that folks need a job now and they are told they need to network, and that isn't helpful.

Another way to do it is to have someone look through your application materials, and then have them practice interview you while looking for gotchas. You want to develop a career history (at least on paper, if not in practice) where you are a successful team member. This is something you want to highlight.

So, when someone says "why are you looking to move on from your current job?" Don't answer by saying anything bad about the current company you are working for. Anything bad may come across as you are the troublemaker, i.e., bad employee. Say something like, "I love my current job, but I have a long commute. I am looking to join a great team like yours, which is much closer to my house." Or maybe, "I worked at Walmart for a couple of years, I learned a lot from my teammates, and now I am ready to take on new challenges as a physicist." Another one might be "Working at Widget Makers was great! They had a real family atmosphere there. It will be hard to leave, but I am looking to grow into a more elite position."

B. Go Get Your Job

When it comes to going and finding a job, it is really important to go get the job. I have been a professor for a while now, and one of the things that I see college graduates do is just do an Indeed search for open jobs and apply to only them. Getting a job this way is very much possible. However, the return on your investment is low. You will apply to a ton of jobs before you hear back and when you do, it is likely that the job you get will be sub-optimal. Of course, doing this is important and you need to do it. In fact, when you try to find jobs in other ways, one of the first things they will ask is that you apply to the job ad online.

Typically, it is good to follow the process when going through the job hunt, and getting that online application in is an important part. But there are other important parts that you are going to need to do to drastically increase your odds.

1. Find someone in the company that you want to work for and ask them about the job. Try to gauge what they are looking for and what problems they have. To find this person you can use LinkedIn to find someone that you are connected to. You might have to ask a mutual connection to introduce you. Be brief (10 minutes, no more) and get to the point. If that person has good information, they will likely give you what they've got, especially if you have a good connection with that person.

2. Do research on the company and find out as much as you can about them. Go to their website and learn about the type of business they do. You should write down questions to ask them. Try to see how your past work and skills align to what they need and do.

3. Tailor your resume (or CV in academics) toward each company you apply to. That's right, that is going to be a lot of work, as you have to do it for every company you apply to. What I find happens when people prepare their application materials is they get it to a point and they think it looks perfect. Then as I am reviewing it, I ask why didn't they make a bigger deal about lasers on the resume; the company you are applying for makes lasers. Then the student says, "I already like how my resume looks, I am not changing it." Obviously, it is their choice, however the opinion of the person who writes a resume is kind of unimportant, it's the opinion of the person who reads the resume that matters. They have to think that your resume is bomb. And if they care about lasers, then your resume should have lasers in it – if you had experience with lasers. Don't lie on a resume. Everything needs to be truthful.

4. Practice your interviews. Go online and you can find things like the top 20 interview questions and such. Take them and customize a few of them to the companies you are applying to. Then practice, practice, practice. I tell my students to have the parents of their girlfriend or boyfriend to ask the questions. I know as a father myself I would love to make the little squirrelly turd that dates my kid squirm with difficult interview questions. Give the interviewer the questions you wrote, and start there. My father-in-law always took it to the next level and asked his own squirmy questions. The squirming is important. You want to work through all of the squirminess so that when you walk in the door you have everything worked out.

5. Dress to impress. You can never overdress for an interview. People may comment on it, but what they say when they are in the smoke-filled rooms is that you really want the job. And that is of course a good thing. If you are unsure, ask the person you talked to about the position. During my first trip to Florida as a management consultant in the summer, my boss told me to dress to the nines and also meet for lunch and make a 1.5 mile walk from the hotel to the business. Everyone laughed at me – everyone else was wearing light, flowing comfortable cloths. I was wearing a full suit! I was the butt of the joke. I was freakin' hot in my suit. But I was still looking sharp when I cooled down and met with the C-level executives, and made a good impression.

6. Be kind to everyone. When we bring someone to campus to interview for a faculty gig, we will often have them on campus for two full days. They meet just about everyone. The person whose opinion I ask for first is our secretary. This type of exchange is usually completely unscripted and it gives a really good idea of how this person will work in our office. If you are unkind to the secrecy, they will let me know, TRUST ME.

7. Follow up with the entire team. Just send a quick email saying something like, "Dear Matt, thank you for showing me your lab during the interview. I am very excited about working at Adelphi, let me know if you have any more questions about me." The person that gets that will not email you back, but it will make them feel like a million bucks! It's always the simple things. You want someone to feel like a million bucks when they think about you.

8. I strongly recommend use helpful resources like the SPS Career Tookbox, which tell you step by step how to get a job. There are resources like this for many different fields and even if you are not a physicist the toolbox is helpful.
https://www.spsnational.org/sites/all/careerstoolbox/

Finding a job is hard. But you got this because you are a freakin' shark!

13 BE A SHARK: THE GAME

I have created a board game which I think helps students practice many of the different concepts you have read about in this book. This is a super fun game that gets people laughing. I have done it at conferences with a 100 people. And to hear everyone laughing and enjoying the game makes me smile.

I tried to build the game off of these simple ideas:

- Showcase how bright you are.
- Get you used to speaking on topics you aren't familiar with.
- Get you used to speaking your mind.
- Building off of other's ideas.
- Putting you at the center of attention.
- Quick decision making.
- Get you making new friends.

Here's how it the game works. You need between 4 and 10 people in a group. Use a random method for selecting one person. You can play odds or evens, or I usually just do 'eeny meeny miny moe'. This person will select the Monarch.

The Monarch has an important job, they do the decision making in the game. Everyone will get a chance to be the Monarch. The first task for the monarch is to select a problem. Here are some examples of some problems:

- How to combat worsting flooding due to global warming
- How to improve student mental health
- How to prevent burnout of Walmart employees during the holiday shopping season

- How can an over-committed student reduce the amount of work they have to do.
- What should the president do about biodiversity loss?
- How should we design a space ship that might go to Mars?
- How can I ask out a friend on a date?

Yea, when I heard a Monarch at a conference once suggest that problem I laughed and laughed and then laughed some more. It works.

The point is the problem can be anything a person wants it to be. It is the Monarch's job to pick.

In the next phase, each player - except for the Monarch - develops their solution on a piece of paper independently. It could be serious, or it could be funny. Usually, the Monarch gives people 2 minutes to develop their idea. The solution can be a short paragraph, a picture, or anything in-between. Creativity is important.

Each of the ideas are folded and put into hat.

Each player – except for the Monarch - randomly picks an idea (e.g., piece of paper). They might get their idea, but probably not.

Then the Monarch selects a player. That player has to give a 1-minute pitch to the Monarch and the rest of the players. This pitch doesn't have to be exactly what was written down on their paper but should be directly inspired by it. The person who is doing the pitch is encouraged to be creative and make the pitch their own.

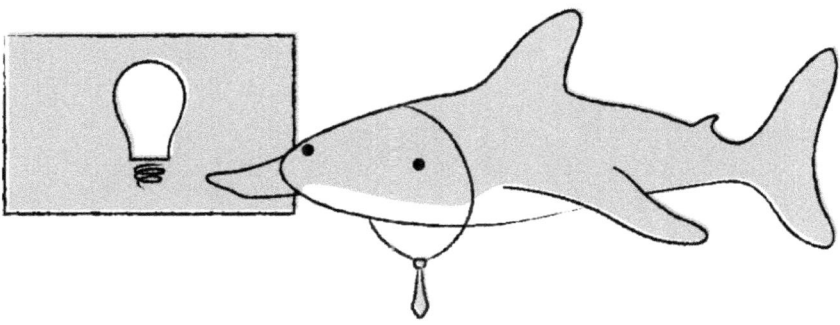

After everyone goes, the Monarch selects the best pitch. The Monarch can ask any follow up question they like. The Monarch gets a point, the person who pitched the idea gets a point, and the person who wrote the idea gets a point.

The Monarch moves clockwise to the next person and you keep playing.

14 CONCLUSION

What are the key takeaways of this book?

Work Hard! Of course, to be a shark you are going to work hard. The best basketball players are the ones that work the hardest. You need to be near the best to be a shark.

Be Hungry! Go out and look for good opportunities, they are not going to find themselves. You have to push to make good things happen.

Be Thorough! Take the time to get the details right. The details matter. A lot. People will knock you down if your details aren't perfect. When you are working through a project, you have to think on different levels. You have to quickly get started (0th order thinking), get it to work (1st order details) and then you have to work out every detail to make sure you understand everything (nth order thinking). This is hard and it takes time. But you have to appease the pushy folks that want results now and the detail orientated people want to make sure everything is accurate and truthful.

Be Fun! Maintain a positive network of people who like you, rely on you, and say nice things about you to anyone who asks.

Of course, this is easy right. Just do all of that and you will be perfect. The only problem is, when do you have time to relax and sleep? Well, you got to do that too. Be you should be a shark about it. Set time to get your work done. When you have reached that goal, drop things and go make sure you spend time with your family, or go to the gym for self-care. And there are going to be times when you just need to sleep in.

You might say that's not very shark-like. But of course, it is. As a wild shark

Be A Shark

you know that there is a limit to what you can do. You may be the fiercest shark in the ocean, but you still aren't going to eat all of the fish at once. It is important to stay well within what is physically possible for you to succeed with what you got. As a wild animal, you don't want to get hurt. Getting hurt is tough because there isn't a hospital for the shark to go to, and the shark is likely going to be permanently damaged and recovery is going to be an issue.

As a shark you want to be healthy and always on the lookout for the next opportunity.

I hope you enjoyed this book. I wish each of you luck on your very sharky path.

Be a shark and remember, da dun da dun da dun.